No More Panic Attacks

A 30-Day Plan for Conquering Anxiety

Jennifer Shoquist M.D. and Diane Stafford

New Page Books
A Division of Career Press Inc.
Franklin Lakes, NJ

NO MORE PANIC ATTACKS
EDITED AND TYPESET BY JOHN J. O'SULLIVAN
Cover design by Lu Rossman/Digi Dog Design
Printed in the U.S.A. by Book-mart Press
Artwork ©2002 *www.arttoday.com*

To order this title, please call toll-free 1-800-CAREER-1 (NJ and Canada: 201-848-0310) to order using VISA or MasterCard, or for further information on books from Career Press.

The Career Press, Inc., 3 Tice Road, PO Box 687,
Franklin Lakes, NJ 07417
www.careerpress.com
www.newpagebooks.com

Library of Congress Cataloging-in-Publication Data

Shoquist, Jennifer.
    No more panic attacks : a 30-day plan for conquering anxiety / by Jennifer Shoquist and Diane Stafford.
        p. cm.
    Includes index.
    ISBN 1-56414-608-1 (pbk.)
        1. Panic attacks--Treatment--Popular works. I. Stafford, Diane. II. Title.

RC535 .S567 2002
616.85'223--dc21

2002069345

Dedication

This book is dedicated with love and gratitude to Belle Shirley,
a woman of tremendous compassion and love.

Love and thanks to our husbands:
Robert San Luis and David Garrett.

Love and thanks to Daddy and Granddaddy,
Clinton Shirley.

And, in loving memory of those who died
in the Attack on America on September 11, 2001.

Acknowledgments

We thank Career Press/New Page Books for believing in our book and allowing us to share our ideas on ways to curb anxiety and live more fulfilling lives. Thanks to our editors at Career Press/New Page: Stacey Farkas, Mike Lewis, and John O'Sullivan. Your hard work and creativity were such important ingredients.

Thank you, Elizabeth Frost-Knappman of New England Publishing Associates, for bringing *No More Panic Attacks* to fruition.

We appreciate the many people who took our 2002 Life Quality Test and offered feedback.

Thanks to our families and friends, who have reduced our anxiety a million times over, kept us targeted on the right priorities, and understood when we had to retreat for many hours into that computer "rabbit hole" to think and work. Your constancy and love make us feel tremendously blessed. Those who were always there with cookies and movies, friendship and love include Martin and Sarah Shoquist, David Nordin, Jennifer Wright, Jami Exner, Chris Fleming, Joanne Goldstein, Leticia San Luis, Allen and Christina Shirley, Austin Shirley, Xanthe Shirley, Lindsay and Cameron Liem, Britt Pierce, Joann Roberson, Donna Pate, Wendy Corson, Camilla and Richard Pierce, Gina and Tom Cartwright, Lina Carlos, Eddi Lee, Carol Ibert, Karen and Doug Johnson, Dinah Anderson, Shari Belmarez, Shannon and John Mathis, Christy Waites, Kristina Holt, Martha Ott, Dana Chandler, Michael Allison, Cari La Grange, Gabriela Baeza Ventura, Gina and Curtis Bradley, Bob Livermore, Fred Aguilar, Tessie Patterson, Rachel Capote, Spiker Davis, Scott Coleman.

We thank Oprah Winfrey, whose vision and beliefs have influenced millions, and we feel lucky to count ourselves among those.

And thanks to David Letterman, who made us laugh, and helped the whole country get back on track after September 11, 2001.

And, thanks to our two adorable, stress-reducing lapdogs: shih-tzus Sophie and Lucy.

Disclaimer

Contents

Preface

Knowing What It's Like
(One Author's Tale of Anxiety)

KNOTS IN YOUR STOMACH. TERROR-GRIP IN YOUR SPINE. A HEART that's beating rat-tat-tat-a-tat so loudly it could wake the dead.

Me? Give a speech? Unthinkable!

First time around, the raw panic response shocked you. What major betrayal from your body! All your anatomical elements were acting out some kind of extreme reaction that resembled Linda Blair in *The Exorcist*. Without having to make eye contact with the audience, you felt sure that fairly disgusting things were dangling out of you—body parts from inside you that you didn't even know were there.

Meanwhile, you stood at the podium, gripping the edges, trying to resemble a normal human being talking to a crowd of people. Through a haze of terror and nausea, you repeated all the old standbys mentally: "Imagine the entire audience sitting out there in their undies. Remember that fear of public speaking is top of the list on America's phobia scale."

But guess what? Nothing helped.

Instead, you heard a trembling voice (read: yours), trying to utter some stumbling bit of nonsense. You felt the oddity of your mouth twitching (easy to imagine how cute that looked). But most riveting of this horrendous display was the beating of your heart, bearing a marked resemblance to the sound of all heavy-metal groups in the world joined together for a concert in your chest, each trying to out-play the others.

This was not okay. Not okay at all.

Your knees buckled. Your mouth turned to cotton. Your eyes sought to dim the whole picture and grant you some perfect exit—like fainting dead, falling from the stage, or beaming into outer space.

Your gut told you that if you ever saw any of these people again, they would look at you with an expression of sad pity—and then you would know just how grotesque your stab at "public speaking" had actually turned out to be. Was this a heart attack at age 25?

Panic attack defined: sheer terror. A place you've been—but don't want to visit ever again.

• • •

If the fright-night situation described above sounds familiar, you probably have the right book in hand. Written by two co-authors who have battled anxiety, this tale started out as a first-person account of a physician's personal victory over panic.

After entering medical school—I, Jennifer Shoquist, a young woman in the male-dominated world of medicine—soon discovered that every time I had to give a presentation, whether it was for doctor-instructors or fellow med students, I'd feel very anxious. Frantically, I looked around for answers so that I'd be able to continue pursuing the work I wanted to do without having any more of these episodes that felt so horribly uncomfortable. Eventually, I found my way.

Now, with co-author Diane Stafford, I share advice on clear-cut ways to handle anxiety and panic obstacles—the many varieties that cause thousands of Americans to live unfulfilling, anxiety-ridden lives.

We want your life to be more peaceful. And, we want to help you get there.

No More Panic Attacks can serve as your guide to dismantling your anxiety disorder—a malady that has evolved as the number-one mental-health plague of this decade.

Even before September 11, 2001, about 19 million Americans suffered from anxiety and panic disorders, with one in 10 having some degree of anxiety associated with mood swings, depression, fatigue, aches and pains, insomnia, and panic attacks. But after the horrendous terrorist acts that revised our basic world view, the umbrella of anxiety suddenly expanded to encompass the entire population, as Americans faced the shroud of insecurity and stress that came with being a country under attack. TV screens were constantly filled with headlines denoting "anthrax anxiety" and "anxiety-ridden Americans under siege," and people began to worry about their ability to cope.

What felt like "going crazy" was really anxiety. And panic. And the endless gut-wrenching fear of the known and the unknown.

However, panic and anxiety can be conquered. Believe it. In this book, we bring you the uplifting message that, in as little as 30 days, you can change negative self-talk to positive can-do skills that promise tremendous health benefits.

Though serious cases of anxiety and panic will often require drug therapy, it is equally important to deal with these debilitating disorders long-term. You will need to use the repertoire of anxiety-busting skills presented here.

We propose a take-charge attitude whereby you learn to squash anxiety with a "hardy-personality" approach. Then, in no time, you'll be bucking adversity with *Indiana Jones* finality.

Change? You may be asking right now if that could possibly be a good thing, after hearing people tell you to "be yourself" all your life. But, if what you're doing isn't working for you, you need to try something else.

In these pages, we share important secrets to ratcheting up your frustration set-point. You will get tools and a 30-day plan of specific steps. We also present 100 nail-biting, stress-inducing scenarios: from dealing with Internet-addicted spouses, maintaining your sanity during company cutbacks, to handling smart-mouthed children, obsessive eating, aging concerns, and fear of biological/chemical warfare. You'll probably relate to some of these dilemmas, and hopefully take away many nuggets that will help you stop the spiral of panic caused by your own personal stressors.

Faulty thinking patterns create symptoms, so an anxious person must learn how to tweak reactions into new forms. You'll learn how to stop being hard on yourself about the fact that you do have trouble handling your panic and anxiety. And, you will learn to simplify your life in ways that will automatically reduce stress levels. You can find your passion and pursue it.

Attitude is everything, which means that learning to reframe situations can help you decrease your anxiety and dilute the effect of stressors. Look at the 45-year-old Houston woman whose skin disease resulted in amputation of both legs, and initially, caused her extreme anxiety. But, knowing she was fortunate to have the backup of very supportive family and friends, she chose to reframe her difficult situation with a positive slant. As an intermediate-school counselor, she labels being wheelchair-bound as an advantage. "The kids see me on their level, and that makes it easier for them to talk to me, and I'm more effective at helping them with their problems." She grins. "I love what I do, and I'm good at it."

Raiding the treasure chest

As you embark on this quest for help and empowerment, get ready for some hard work. It is going to take courage and optimism. You have to revise your way of thinking about yourself and the way you deal with those around you. You have to improve your self-image and stop cowering. Stop presuming everyone is right but you. Gaining a hardy personality is oh-so-do-able.

You'll switch from negative self-talk to positive, can-do mantras that have amazing benefits. You'll get rid of habits that aren't getting you anywhere, and replace them with new and better behaviors. You *can* become calmer and happier. And you can do it in as little as 30 days. Get ready to subdue your fears and live passionately.

Just keep your goal in sight—living free of panic and fear and claiming the Good Life that you so richly deserve. It's out there!

Introduction

Simple Stress, Panic, or Anxiety Disorder?

YOUR HEART IS BEATING RAPIDLY. YOUR THROAT FEELS TIGHT. YOU'RE afraid something bad may happen. Terrified, you confide in someone, only to have your complaints dismissed as being crazy, an exaggeration, or hypochondria.

You think you've had a panic attack, but people just say you're faking or overreacting. This spurs you to do the opposite of what you need to do, which is seek treatment. You figure, "They're right and I'm wrong—I'm just being silly. So what if my heart races? And my palms are sweaty? And I feel breathless? I'm just being a freak."

Although many people will tell you that such problems are psychosomatic (in your head), and that you'd feel better if you would *just try*, the truth of the matter is that panic attacks are very real. You've probably tried hard to stop them, but your attempts didn't work. You can't sweep the problem under the carpet without addressing the cause and finding out what you can do to prevent panic attacks in the future. If friends, family, and sometimes even doctors tell you that all you need to do is "straighten up," but *you know* that something's seriously wrong, *ignore them* and listen to your body. Get help! Most folks simply can't relate to the stark terror of a panic attack and the discomfort and irrationality of these dark moments because they haven't been there.

By the same token, though, you *have* been there—and you'll be thrilled to hear that a panic or anxiety disorder is very treatable. Why live with the torment?

Are you having "normal" stress, or panic attacks?

Make no mistake, panic attacks are indeed "mental disturbances"—a fact you know all too well if you've suffered from them. However, don't confuse "normal" stress with a true disorder. You can live with occasional bouts of stomach-butterflies.

Simple "stress" may cause physical symptoms, but lots of folks thrive under stress. Some even excel thanks to the persistent push of stress. On the other hand, stress that comes from psychological or emotional factors can result in insomnia, lack of focus, anxiety, weight gain or loss, general malaise, and digestive distress. Long-term stress can weaken the immune system, and may contribute to heart disease, high blood pressure, and headaches.

To differentiate between "normal" stress, and the kind that disarms and causes panic attacks, let's look at a reference point—the veil of uncertainty that covered all Americans in the months following the September 11th terrorist attacks. Many people wondered whether they were behaving normally and having average reactions, considering the gravity of the problem. Or were their symptoms signs of a full-fledged anxiety disorder? Hosts of talk shows tossed the subject around, observing that people were exhibiting a wide range of emotional turmoil in their behavior patterns.

Check yourself out

Thinking back to the period following September 11, try to recall your reactions. Were you fragmented and grief-stricken for a few weeks or months, after which you reluctantly resumed your former routine? Or did the gloom stick with you for so long that it became crippling?

Look at the following descriptions, and decide which one most closely represents the things you did during that time of extreme duress:

1. You felt extremely sad, unfocused, and scattered. You had uncertainty about the security of your life and that of your family, and you spent a great deal of time pondering these issues. Sometimes you cried. You couldn't drag yourself away from the television coverage of the atrocities. You gave blood and donated money. The only way you could make yourself feel better was to eat everything in sight and shop for new security devices, equipping yourself for the worst-case scenario. This didn't really decrease your stress, but you began to view that stress as your post-tragedy reality. For months, grief gnawed at you at unexpected times and diminished your peace of mind significantly.

2. You felt as if the world would never be the same, and you began to abandon things you had previously planned: a change of profession, attempts to get pregnant, a big trip. You sank lower and lower into despondency and lethargy. Experiencing ongoing anxiety, you refused to go anywhere except work. At least, if you were going to die, you probably would be at home. You decided to be angry forever. You vowed to cling to your grief, in honor of the victims. Life was ruined for you. At work, your sales figures plummeted. You began to miss work, showing up erratically, if at all. You were angry with your coworkers, whose grieving did not meet your standards. You related totally to the "anthrax anxiety" being discussed on TV, and you knew that soon you would be inhaling the deadly substance. It was only a matter of time before your number was up.

3. At first, you had serious doubts that the world would ever return to anything resembling normalcy, and you worried that you would never feel safe again. You found it hard to do your regular work. The only things that seemed to make you feel better were talks with friends and family. Then, a clear vision emerged, showing you that the only way to make any sense of the tragedy was to let it fuel your desire to maximize your time on earth. You went back to work, trying to get on with your life, and found ways to get outside of your sorrow by extending yourself, helping others, and living with greater passion. You took the enormous reserve of energy that

mounted up during the emotional crisis and funneled it into productive outlets. You began doing volunteer work. You started attending church regularly for the first time in years.

Clearly, these are only three of many possible reactions to the September 11th catastrophes. But, if you saw yourself in responses one and three, your level of stress could be rated "normal" in terms of this horrific set of circumstances. We all have unsettling stressors in our lives; we all cope with these, some of us more effectively than others. Usually we muddle our way through them. Stress annoys us like a gnat in our eye, but it doesn't drag us down.

The person in example three had the healthiest response. This person took adversity and made it an incentive to make life count even more. The person in number one was more like, "hey, I lived through it so I'll just keep a low profile." This is an approach that lacks gusto, but at least it is more survivor-like than number two.

The individual in example number two, obviously steeped in chronic anxiety, felt totally undone and incapacitated by the crisis. This probably wasn't the first time that this person had been wracked with anxiety. To get through the quicksand, this individual needs to find a way to dismantle irrational thoughts—one of the skills that anyone with an anxiety disorder must learn in order to achieve greater peace of mind.

Let's look at the previous assumptions and dissect them. This method is one of many that you'll soon be tucking into your skill-set for anxiety-busting:

I will never feel secure again

Let's be honest: If someone did feel perfectly secure prior to the catastrophe, it was certainly false security. The world was already a dangerous place. If you weren't acknowledging that, you simply were gliding along in denial.

I will be mad forever, and anger just makes me exhausted and incapable of doing much

Anger *is* real, and a person should acknowledge those feelings. But, you could also turn that into potent energy and use it to do something—rather than cower in self-pity. You know without a doubt that those who died in the Pennsylvania, Pentagon, and World Trade Center horrors would not want their deaths to turn Americans into pale, sad versions of their former selves.

I will abandon all my plans because who knows if I'll be around to do them

This shows why you should postpone all major decision-making to a future time of less turmoil. A crisis period is an awful time to try to make major life decisions. Far better to let some time go by, and then take out your options and view them with a cooler, less-frenzied eye. Perhaps the world won't ever be the same again—you could be right. But that's no excuse to stop trying to make the most of your life.

I can't find anything that makes me feel safe; living feels virtually hopeless

Increasing safety measures can make you feel safer. At the same time, you don't want to turn into the King or Queen of Surveillance and Security. Living in fear isn't what you're here to do.

My life seems totally insignificant in the scope of the tragedy. I'm just a computer professional. Besides, when I go to work, it makes me mad that others are going about their lives and not grieving properly

Wrong. You *are* significant. Every single person's contribution to society does matter. All of us must continue to contribute in the ways that we did prior to the life-altering horror, and align ourselves with the steely philosophy that no one wants evil men to decimate the fabric of American life.

As for your yen to "rate" the grieving of others, that's not yours to do. Everyone grieves in his or her own way, and that's absolutely okay. Instead of being hard on others, scrutinize yourself. Are the things you're doing with your life worthwhile? If not, it could be time to work on making changes, ramping up your value.

I get myself so worked up about my misery that I have panic attacks: my heart races, I can't breathe, and I feel like I'm going to die

Feeling frightened by what happened on September 11th is quite rational. But, it's not rational to let it fill you with anxiety for a year or more. You could probably benefit from professional counseling if you're feeling this way.

What to expect of yourself after a crisis

After a crisis, you need to reestablish a sense of order and balance. Try to be aware of the difference between reactions that are reasonable, given the scope of the tragedy, and ones that are not-so-reasonable, and life-damaging. When your grieving becomes toxic to you and to others, seek help and get outside of yourself. Give comfort to others, and envision a time when you'll grieve less and enjoy life more. Build on your closeness with friends and family. Refuse to make big decisions for a couple of months, and resume normal activities as soon as possible. Confusion is normal; but not even trying to live is corrosive.

As talk-show host David Letterman said the night he sadly returned to his post after the events of September 11, "There's only one requirement for any of us—and that's to be courageous, and pretending to be courageous is just as good as the real thing." Thousands of viewers could relate. He became an ambassador of American patriotism and spirit with his amazing display of emotion that moved all of us who felt like displaced citizens. Within a week, Letterman was making us laugh—and most of us were trying to find a way to jumpstart our old selves. You deal with stressors by handling them, whether you like them or not.

But a full-fledged anxiety disorder, on the other hand, is not so easily resolved. Pulling yourself up by bootstraps doesn't work. Obviously, if the resolution were that simple, you wouldn't see a fourth of our population walking around with anxiety disorders.

Asking for help

Sadly, few people who have this problem do seek treatment, but you don't have to suffer in silence, or become dysfunctional. Here in your hands—in this book—is your chance to discover if what you're experiencing is anxiety or a panic disorder. And to find a way to get better.

If you do go in for medical help, give your doctor specifics about your condition. Many people offer vague complaints that don't help a physician zero in on the problem. Lacking specific information, your doctor may tell you that you're "just fine" physically, which will leave you feeling strange and paranoid. If a doctor views your problem with skepticism, you'll conclude, "Okay, he's right, I'm wrong. I'm making a mountain out of a molehill. I'll be just fine." That works until you have another panic attack and get scared witless once again.

All too often, a panic sufferer just accepts fate with no treatment, and lets others write her off as "high-strung" or "a nervous wreck." She feels silly, having such a hazy kind of ailment, and can see why others discount her complaints as overblown—perhaps, even as cries for attention. At any rate, the panic-attack victim may feel like no one seems to know how to help. Friends and family just keep spouting that unhelpful old saw about "pulling yourself up by the bootstraps." Clearly, they're missing the most important point: If you were capable of "fixing" yourself, by now you would have done it!

When you have the "Disorder of the Decade"

Disturbing or debilitating symptoms tell you that you're probably suffering from anxiety or a panic disorder, and that puts you in the company of hordes of fellow sufferers. Anxiety disorders are the most common of all emotional disorders, according to the National Institute of Mental Health, the federal agency that conducts and supports research related to mental disorders, mental health, and the brain. In fact, these maladies are so widespread that mental health experts have named social anxiety the "Disorder of the Decade."

Some people are so paralyzed by anxiety that it keeps them from trying new things, taking trips, even doing simple things like riding the subway or going on elevators. Others become so crippled that it is virtually impossible for them to talk to their bosses, give presentations, or ask for dates. Of the 19 million Americans who suffer from anxiety and panic disorders, many admit that they rarely see a glimmer of hope, much less imagine any kind of joie de vivre.

Finding something to make the panic go away

Anxiety sends some people to doctors for solutions. They may get Paxil or Prozac, beta-blockers or BuSpar. For many, drug therapy is effective, which has made medications for chronic anxiety the most routinely prescribed drugs in our society. Drugs such as Zoloft, Ativan, and Xanax are used to treat millions of people.

Unfortunately, reliance on drugs can make people postpone dealing with their issues. And of the 30 million-plus who take anxiety- and panic-curbing medications, more than four million are addicted. However, only certain types of antianxiety medicines are considered to have addictive potential. Some physicians think that these specific drugs (the benzodiazepines) only aggravate the very conditions they're designed to remedy, as they can create a spiral effect. The sufferer seeks the medication, uses it to get through the specified stressor, but then finds it impossible to tackle that stressor or similar ones without the aid of medication. This can stir up even more anxiety; the individual becomes so reliant on the drug that the mere thought of approaching the "angst situation" without a mood-smoothing medication cranks up the stress to even higher levels. Obviously, this roller-coaster effect is bad for your health.

Used with or without drug therapy, your best option for coping with long-term anxiety is learning new ways to respond to your fears. Behavior-modification therapy—changing your reactions to things that frighten you—can have life-altering effects. You can learn to use "panic-handling" skills routinely with or without anxiety and panic medication. What you need depends on the severity of your problem. If yours is crippling, you'll definitely need to have a physician's help in setting up your plan because you'll probably require medication at the outset of treatment.

The American Psychiatric Association reports that more than 19 million Americans experience anxiety-disorder symptoms. These include overwhelming feelings of panic and fear, uncontrollable obsessive thoughts, intrusive memories, recurring nightmares, and physical reactions (nausea, migraines, muscle tension, sweating, among others). Often, these problems pop up unexpectedly—seemingly without any reason—and hang around to create disturbances. In other people, there's a specific trigger—a feared situation or thing.

To figure out if you have an anxiety or panic malady (or something else), review the descriptions below to discover the name of the disorder that's causing you trouble:

Check out these "disconnects"

Panic disorder

Fear stalks you. When you think you're in danger, you can have chest pain, heart-pounding, sweating, trembling, shortness of breath, nausea or stomach pain, dizziness, numbness or chills, a feeling of choking, and a general "disconnect." You may actually believe that you are about to die or "go nuts." In most cases, your panic attacks hit with no warning, and at times, you may fear that you could be having a heart attack. Rushing to the E.R. is not an unusual reaction to the scary feeling of a panic attack.

Also, you may have weeks of extreme concern about having another attack, or you may have altered your behavior as a result of the attack. Or you've spent a lot of time worrying about what the attack means (you suspect serious disease or mental illness). You may also have trouble with depression (about half of those who have panic attacks suffer from depression).

Using cocaine, amphetamines, or excessive caffeine may result in high anxiety that mimics panic attacks—also a possibility if you're undergoing physiologic withdrawal from alcohol or drugs. Some over-the-counter weight-loss products, too, contain ephedrine or other agents that pump up anxiety sensations. Some of the medical conditions that have the same symptoms as panic disorder are hypoxia, pulmonary embolism, hyperthyroidism, and cardiac arrhythmias.

Often, a person who's experiencing a mild case of panic disorder responds well to behavior modification, especially when he or she can learn relaxation techniques that work and gain an understanding of what the symptoms mean (and what they don't mean). But, if panic attacks result in major distress and are disabling, affecting work, home, or social life, your best bet is probably drug therapy combined with behavioral changes.

Many physicians treat panic and anxiety disorders with medications and cognitive-behavioral therapy. Cognitive therapy can alter the thought patterns that contribute to your rising panic, and behavioral therapy helps you move your patterns in more positive directions.

If you have panic attacks, you probably have some distorted (exaggerated) thoughts—overblown fears that give rise to the cycle of growing anxiety that leads to a panic attack set in motion by a few seconds of sensations that spiral. It usually starts with increased heart rate, a tight chest, or a feeling of nausea. You become more anxious, which makes you feel worse. Then you get scared; you must be having a heart attack or going insane! The vicious cycle has precipitated a panic attack.

Panic disorder typically starts in late teen years or early adulthood, and rarely does a person suddenly develop panic attacks in his 40s or later.

Phobias

A phobia is a strong but irrational fear of a certain situation, activity, or object. In most people, phobias are diagnosed only when the problem has progressed to such a disabling extent that normal functioning is difficult or impossible.

A person with a *specific phobia* knows the fear is irrational but is unable to overcome it. An object or situation causes an uncontrollable feeling of wanting to avoid it at all costs. Sometimes the individual with a phobia doesn't know what makes him or her feel this way—the only certainty is that the fear is huge.

Social phobia (or social anxiety disorder) refers to strong anxiety surrounding a fear of social or performance situations (parties, public speaking, and so forth). You think you will be embarrassed, so you just avoid the situation altogether. If you are forced to go ahead and enter the arena that frightens you, the discomfort you feel may be almost unbearable.

One anxiety-ridden man (Ronnie*) wondered lifelong why other people seemed happy because he had *never* felt like that. He was terminally gloomy and felt panicky in social situations. He felt

*All the names in this book were changed to protect each person's anonymity.

self-conscious speaking in front of groups and even eating in front of people. At 45, when he finally became sick of watching others bypass him professionally and personally, he sought psychiatric help and was put on an antianxiety/antidepressant medication. Ronnie also learned behavior-modification techniques. On several occasions, the doctor changed medications until they settled on the best solution. At last, this man was able to discover why other people sometimes seemed so joyful.

"The drugs 'evened me out' and lifted my spirits," Ronnie explained. "For the first time in my life, I felt like smiling. Situations that used to freak me out lost their power over me. I don't feel perfect, but I'm definitely better."

Agoraphobia, a debilitating problem that turns some people into hermits, is based on the individual's belief that he or she will be put in a situation that's embarrassing or hard to escape. Working from that belief system, you take the logical approach: you simply stay at home.

Social phobia and agoraphobia can appear hand in hand with panic disorder. Avoiding public places and situations may seem like the perfect solution, or the only one, for those who believe they can't depend on their own ability to stem the rising tide of fears and panic. Although the agoraphobic individual doesn't want to go out in public, the social phobic takes it a step further, conjuring up scary scenarios in which every action is scrutinized and criticized by others outside the home. The victim is in the clutches of a crippling shyness, and doesn't want to try to socialize with other people because of overwhelming fears of social failure.

One of the saddest things about a phobia is that even though logic will remind you that the fear is totally illogical, you're still hamstrung–home seems like the only safe zone. Your fears get bigger and bigger, and you may become convinced that the only answer is staying out of elevators, or never driving, or avoiding whatever your fear-trigger is. Sadly, unless you get help to find your way out of this maze of confusing input, you will tiptoe through life, blindfolded and handcuffed by your fears.

Obsessive-compulsive disorder

Of anxiety disorders, OCD often strikes outsiders as the oddest of mental disorders. If you're not an OCD sufferer, you will probably be a bit baffled when your friend needs to rewash his hands over and over—or go back to his house to double-check to see that the oven is off. This person's intensely "anal" attitude toward hand-washing, oven-checking, and germ-avoiding can make him the butt of jokes. But this problem is anything but amusing to the one caught in the throes of it. Someone with OCD lives with repetitive rituals that take time and make daily functioning cumbersome. Unfortunately, left untreated, OCD can progress until obsessive thoughts or compulsive behaviors rule the sufferer's life—they can't be controlled rationally.

Some people who have obsessive-compulsive disorder follow complex rituals, while others hoard collections of odd things of no value. Because many OCD folks know that their thoughts or behaviors seem nonsensical, they'll usually hide the problem rather than seek help. The fact is, behavior modification and medications can help curb this disorder. If you obsess about something to the point that you must do it compulsively, and this ritual is disrupting your life or that of your family—you need to get help.

Post-traumatic stress disorder

You've gone through a horrifying event, and the last thing you'd like to do is visit it again. But that's your fate: revisiting it time after time. Your flashbacks may be accompanied by extreme distress, with symptoms such as difficulty sleeping, depression, edginess, and a general case of the jitters. Events that generally trigger PTSD initially are rape, military combat, natural disasters, abuse, divorce (especially if your spouse was abusive or an alcohol or drug abuser), and tragedies (such as the September 11th terrorist attacks).

A person with PTSD can walk away from trauma with such deeply etched emotional numbness that, without treatment, he or she can become immune to feeling joy or sadness, as if an emotional light bulb has simply gone out. Sometimes, PTSD sufferers have such vivid nightmares and flashbacks that they're forced to endure their horrible trauma repeatedly, which can cause life-altering disruption. A sound or a word can throw the person off kilter, making the victim want to shut himself or herself off from family and friends in order to cope.

Consider Susanna*: She could still be jarred in a staggering way by the sound of ice cubes falling into a glass, even though 20 years had passed since she divorced an abusive alcoholic. In an instant, her mind and emotions would transcend time and space and shoot back to mornings when the first sound she heard upon waking was ice cubes falling into a glass, as her husband fixed his first drink of the day. Like ice-pick stabs, the painful emotions came rushing back, causing her to stave off the painful memories with a shroud of numbness. She grew so disturbed by this that she felt nothing emotionally. In relationships with men, Susanna sensed an odd distancing that she couldn't understand until she was finally able to identify the trigger.

She usually dated men who drank, and as soon as she heard drinks being prepared, she would retreat emotionally. She couldn't be hurt because her heart and mind wouldn't let her reenter the fray of real feeling and emoting. In her hideaway, she would stay safe. But she would never be happy.

• • •

One of the strangest aspects of this disorder is that the symptoms can occur years after the event. A classic example is sexual abuse, which the sufferer sometimes fails to address (or even admit) for decades. Because horror and shame are attached to sexual abuse, a person may confront what happened to her only when the symptoms of post-traumatic stress disorder become debilitating, and thus, pinpointing the cause becomes absolutely necessary. (Consider the cases of sexual abuse now rife in the Catholic Church, many of which involve adults who are finally addressing their pain 20 or 30 years after the fact.)

Post-traumatic stress disorder gives the affected person an unwanted rerun of the traumatic sexual abuse, thus making her avoid anything that will spur bad memories of the way she felt at the time, and the way she feels about it currently. A pattern of avoidance develops, accompanied by emotional numbness. The unsettling recollections of PTSD can result in restrained emotions, a sense of doom, and an angst-like detachment from others sometimes described as a "disconnect."

For generally healthy people who have been experiencing PTSD symptoms for less than six months, there's a good chance of complete recovery if—and this is an important if—they don't have other disorders (drug or alcohol addiction, medical or psychiatric problems), and they also have a good support system of relatives and friends.

If you suffer from PTSD, your doctor will probably prescribe a medication, and recommend that you use relaxation techniques. For some who have PTSD, hypnosis works well.

Generalized anxiety disorder

Generalized anxiety disorder (GAD) is a common culprit behind physical and emotional difficulties. Physicians see GAD frequently.

These people live with constant worry and are always jumpy and edgy. Friends might describe someone with GAD as being "in a snit" most of the time. These individuals spend their days in a wrought-up, worried state, even if most of their concerns may be wildly overblown, having no foundation in fact. Sometimes, the concerns actually are valid ones, such as worrying about money, marriage, children, or health. Generalized anxiety disorder differs from panic disorder in that a person with GAD is a chronic worrier, whereas the panic-attack person experiences intermittent terror, as well as a great deal of anxiety in anticipating another panic attack.

One GAD sufferer, the mother of a 28-year-old, admitted she obsessed 24 hours a day, seven days a week, about her son's safety. Her son is a stockbroker who lives in an apartment, goes to work every day, and has a normal life. However, his mom got upset at the sound of every ambulance siren in the distance because she figured it was going to pick up her son, who had fallen victim to disaster. She knows it's not logical when she speaks of her problem, but the nagging fears were relentless. She experienced trembling, muscle aches, dry mouth, and was easily startled.

If you have GAD, you have frequent and extreme anxiety. You worry about events or activities much of the time for at least six months. The worry is hard to control and hampers your functioning in the workplace, home, or in social situations. You also have three or more of these symptoms most of the time for six months (in children, only one symptom is needed to make the problem GAD): restlessness, muscle aches, fatigue, sleep disturbances, irritability, and difficulty concentrating.

Folks with GAD obsess about bad outcomes that might befall themselves, friends, relatives, jobs, or finances. (They're often known as worriers.) Each morning, the GAD person feels his worries starting all over again. About a quarter of those with GAD develop panic disorder.

Substance-abuse-related anxiety disorder is a special situation in which a person can feel anxious from amphetamine or cocaine use, or from consuming too much caffeine. Also, a person who is withdrawing from alcohol or a benzodiazepine (such as Xanax) may have anxiety symptoms. When your doctor takes your medical history and possibly even does a toxicology screen, he'll find out if he can exclude the possibility that your GAD arises from a substance-abuse problem. It is also important to note that a patient who has a psychiatric disorder, including a mood or psychotic disorder, will often have marked anxiety. However, this is not GAD unless the anxiety is unrelated to the other disorders.

Your doctor also will look for a disease or health condition that could give rise to anxiety symptoms. Some of these are cardiac arrhythmias, pulmonary embolism, congestive heart failure, hypoglycemia, and hyperthyroidism.

So, what's your problem?

Brain chemistry, genetics, and life experiences all play roles in anxiety disorders. Your basic personality also figures into the mix. People with low self-esteem cope with adversity more poorly than confident types. However, researchers and physicians have learned a great deal about the mechanics of these disorders, paving the way for doctors to delineate the markers of each problem, and come up with appropriate treatments that work.

Until these disorders were acknowledged as real and legitimate health problems, they were medical stepchildren. Then, when they suddenly became more recognized, the door was opened for doctors to provide evaluation and treatment for panic sufferers. From there, medical professionals proceeded to make anxiety disorders the "big kahuna," and then list underneath, its entire spectrum of problems:

panic disorder, obsessive-compulsive disorder, phobias, generalized anxiety disorder, and post-traumatic stress disorder.

With the help of your doctor, you can pinpoint what your trouble is. Don't hesitate to look for answers, and refuse to let someone tell you that you're "fine" when you know that's not the case.

Left untreated, an anxiety disorder can cripple you. The pattern often spurs an intense dread of social interaction that teaches the sufferer to avoid the terror-filled experience and thus, end up confined to a safe haven (home). Personal relationships and work performance suffer because it's hard to be a good companion or employee when your life revolves around avoiding things.

However, we bring you magnificent news: If you "take the treatment" for an anxiety or panic disorder, you can find relief. In about 70 to 90 percent of those with panic disorder, treatment works.

We're ready to lead you down a road to recovery so you can celebrate life to a spectacular degree once again.

1

Anxiety, Up-Close and Personal

WAKING UP TO MY BEEPER'S HEAD-BANGING ASSAULT, I TRIED TO focus my tired, bloodshot eyes on my bleak surroundings—a hospital on-call room. I looked around and reached for a piece of stale bagel. Hunger pangs tickled my gut. From outside the room, I heard the bustling sounds of nurses and patients. I smelled disinfectant. Apparently, the night cleanup crew had come and gone, and I was in such a deep sleep I never even knew it.

I looked up and saw a way-too-cheerful face. Sticking his head in the door, a grinning first-year med student was looking to me, of all people, for guidance. Stressors hit full tilt. As a third-year resident in family practice, I was facing the remaining 12 hours of a 36-hour hospital stint, fueled by three hours' sleep in two days. My hair was hanging in grizzled ringlets around my face, and all I had in the way of resources to spiff myself up was a tiny bathroom and my toothbrush and toothpaste. I had three minutes to get myself ready to show up in the hall, out in public, looking and sounding chipper (at best) and, if that failed, lucid (at worst). I stumbled out of the narrow bed, and found my black clogs nearby.

Then I remembered I was facing a presentation that would be in the presence of male doctors who rated me daily. And this talk had to be done, regardless of the fact that I had a fear of public speaking. "Why am I doing this?" I asked myself.

This is anxiety. Dealing with stress makes us stronger; we can use it to amp us up to perform better, soar to greater heights. But dealing with anxiety, on the other hand, just makes us feel crazy.

I knew I wasn't alone. My dilemma during medical school and residency was one that many people face in all realms of life every day of the week—19 million Americans, to be exact. Anxiety. Panic.

Many times, anxiety froze me, and I felt like I wasn't going to be able to give that speech, or "present" that patient to a group of residents, or please that demanding professor. Sometimes I trembled; other times, I felt breathless. Frequently, I felt certain that I really didn't have what it took to make it through medical school and residency. As shy as I had been growing up, I simply wasn't equipped to compete with the level of "swagger" that's necessary in medicine, which remains very much a male bastion. So, I had to find answers, or give it all up. I reminded myself that I'd put in too many years of grueling study to let crippling fits of anxiety wreck my life, but I couldn't figure out what to do.

I eventually set out the problem in clear-cut terms: "Jennifer, either get a handle on your anxiety—get to the bottom of it—or you're looking at a life lacking peace. Overall happiness will elude you because you'll be too busy untying the knots in your psyche to enjoy life fully."

What seems like grand irony, especially considering my "anxiety history," is that many patients I see in my family-medicine practice suffer from anxiety and/or panic attacks.

Harking back to the not-so-good-old-days

Believe me, I know what you're feeling!

In a heartbeat, I can summon up that old familiar sense of dread that turns the heart into a jackhammer. For example, one time when I walked into a gross anatomy lab, I knew it was the day my attending doctor (who was my supervisor) was going to hit me with a barrage of questions. Borrowing the grief in advance of the dreaded experience, I began perspiring. Soon I felt dizzy and my heart was racing.

And, then I learned to pick apart the panic attack, step by step. In analyzing the situation, I remembered that I had been obsessing even before I arrived about my knowledge compared to that of my peers, who often seemed to know more. I pounded myself with negative self-talk: *"They study more and are better informed on the material we're supposed to know. I know I'll be humiliated today because I won't know the answers. I am such a misfit because all the others know exactly what they want. The doctor evaluating me will notice that I am ill-prepared and will judge me."*

In retrospect, studying the negative thoughts, I saw why I felt so anxious. I went from feeling bad to feeling worse. And I was the one brewing up the awful thoughts—not anyone else! In fact, I never once experienced ridicule at the hand of an instructor. However, I was plagued by the belief (and panicky feeling) that soon, it was going to happen. It was, in fact, long overdue.

A helpful technique when a recurring situation makes you anxious is scrutinizing the entire chain of thoughts. Try to figure out what caused the low, worrisome mood. Jot down how you felt and what stirred that feeling. Eventually, this insight will help you understand what sets off your bouts of anxiety, making you better able to cope.

What I found was that the very thoughts that seemed to make sense in my head looked totally ridiculous and illogical on paper. Having pinpointed my distorted thoughts, I was able to move them into my consciousness. There, I could work on altering them.

Monitoring self-talk soon became a habit. I increased my self-confidence by practicing positive mantras that said, "So what if someone knows more than I do, and so what if I answer a question wrong?" Look at the blackest possible outcome of any situation, and generally, you'll find that it is something you can deal with. It may not be what you would like to have happen, but it's not the apocalypse, either.

Consider the possibility that your colleagues are also afraid, poorly prepared, or unfocused. Remind yourself that the formidable-world-against-you theory is not an accurate perception. Just like you, the smartest kid in your class or coworker at your job has off days when he or she fails to perform at his best—and that's all right. No one should expect to be a prime performer every single moment of every day—it's a false and overly demanding expectation. (By the way, avoid the clichéd practice of telling your child daily "do your best," because it sends the message that you expect her to be peak-performing all the time, and she can only fall short of that expectation. Far better to tell her to enjoy her day.) Of course, it's fine to encourage your child to do well, but you don't want her to think that she has to be operating at 100 percent all of the time. Being at the top of her game consistently simply won't happen, and she may worry about disappointing you.

Understanding social anxiety

Maybe you're like me—you hate to be under the magnifying glass. But, at the same time, you consider yourself fairly sociable. Does that make sense?

It should. One of today's most common types of anxiety disorders is *social phobia*, and the person who suffers from this problem isn't always shy. In fact, you may feel very much at ease with people, but certain situations can cause you intense anxiety. Even an outgoing person can suffer from social phobia, which is an enormous fear of being humiliated or embarrassed in social situations. Typically, this begins in childhood when you develop a faulty belief system based on self-doubt. You assume other people are competent, but you, in contrast, aren't. This can make you blush, fumble, and feel as if every eye is evaluating you critically.

Sometimes, your anxiety grows to the point that you actually experience chest pains, sweaty palms, dry mouth, increased heart rate, lightheadedness, dizziness, diarrhea, or frequent urination. Or, you may have symptoms that aren't listed here—ones that are uniquely your own.

Social anxiety disorder is so commonplace that mental health professionals have labeled it "the neglected anxiety disorder," meaning that it's often missed in diagnosis. People want to shrug off anxiety as no big deal. It's almost as taboo as talking about sexually transmitted diseases, menopause, or impotence. Everyone knows about these things, but they're tough to talk about.

Physicians can treat social anxiety disorder, but unfortunately, they see a substantial rate of relapse even after prolonged treatment. Evidence suggests, however, that patients who receive cognitive-behavioral therapy in addition to medication, may have lower rates of relapse. Early and aggressive treatment of social anxiety disorder may prevent development of associated disorders and can substantially improve quality of life.

Sometimes, social phobia gets totally out of hand. Fear of a certain situation provokes anxiety, resulting in a panic attack from fear of the situation. You have ongoing trepidation about a social situation in which you will be exposed to people you don't know. Or you fear people will scrutinize you, and you will be embarrassed. You may realize that your fear is excessive, but you avoid the situation, anyway—or endure it with extreme anxiety. You may have what is called "generalized social anxiety" if you happen to be afraid of almost all social encounters: conversations, dating, parties, speaking to authority figures, among others.

What that mountain looks like

Over and beyond the social anxiety that's fairly ordinary, however, is the mighty panic attack. And you may know all too well what that feels like.

You're climbing Panic Mountain, but not because you want to plant a flag at the top, or "just because it's there." Your Everest came to you unbidden in the form of panic attacks, and now you're stuck with the job of trying to figure out how to mount and subdue it, once and for all. "Straightening up"—the advice friends may offer—isn't going to resolve panic attacks.

Specifically defined by the American Psychiatric Association's *Diagnostic and Statistical Manual of Mental Disorders, fourth edition (DSM-IV)*, a panic attack is "a period of intense fear or discomfort in which four or more symptoms developed abruptly and reached a peak within 10 minutes." The *DSM-IV* lists common symptoms: sweating, shortness of breath, numbness or tingling, sensations of choking, palpitations or accelerated heart rate, trembling, chest pain, nausea, dizziness or lightheadedness, fear of losing control or going crazy, fear of dying, and chills or hot flashes. No special stimulus kicks off these symptoms, and the attacks are sudden and brief—usually, minutes. Then they go away without the sufferer having done anything. This attack is a surprise to you.

To fit the diagnostic definition of panic disorder, you must have had recurrent unexpected attacks, and at least a month of anxiety about having another attack; or a month or more of worry about the consequences or implications of panic attacks; or a month or more of a significant change that you made because of your near-debilitating fear of having panic attacks. Also, the attacks must not be related to the effects of drug abuse, a medication you're taking, or a medical condition such as hyperthyroidism.

Sometimes, panic disorder is associated with irritable bowel syndrome, vomiting, and abdominal pain. You may fear having uncontrollable diarrhea or be afraid of losing bladder or bowel control. You can't go anywhere that lacks a handy toilet. And, although the possibility of having a heart attack due to panic is medically unfounded, the fear of losing bowel control is sometimes realized under extreme stress. And that sets up a cycle of fear.

Migraines are yet another problem. Some panic-attack sufferers have migraine headaches so painful that they worry about having a stroke. A survey of 10,000+ people found that women diagnosed with panic disorder reported headaches that were more severe and lasted longer than the migraines experienced by women who do not have panic disorder. A staggering 20 to 40 percent found their headaches disabling.

Doctor, doctor, give me the news!

By now, you may have already seen a doctor. But if you haven't, you *need* to go in for a physical examination so that your physician can rule out the possibility of a medical condition (other than anxiety) that could be producing your symptoms. You'll probably walk away with a prescription to curb panic symptoms and, hopefully, prevent more attacks. And, if you don't get relief from what you're prescribed or what the doctor recommends, keep searching for answers. You may want to find a doctor who regularly handles panic and anxiety disorders.

The National Institutes of Health offers the following guidelines for finding a physician to treat anxiety:

- Follow the leader. If your physician doesn't treat anxiety disorder, he or she may refer you to a mental health professional, such as a psychiatrist. Psychologists, social workers, and counselors can't write prescriptions, but they often work closely with a primary care physician or psychiatrist, who can prescribe necessary medications.
- Choose someone who knows cognitive-behavioral or behavioral therapy, and who is open to the use of medication, if that is necessary.
- Ask the professional you're considering what kinds of therapy he or she generally uses, and whether medications are available. You need to feel comfortable with the kind of therapy you will receive.
- Get your physician's help in tapering off an anxiety medication (if that's necessary).
- Look for a healthcare professional you like because you'll be working as a team.

Unfortunately, some doctors think panic-attack patients are neurotic when their medical tests don't show signs of any physical problem. However, panic symptoms are very real, certainly not imagined, and they feel life-threatening. Fortunately, with the right treatment, panic attacks can be managed well, and often eliminated entirely.

No doubt, considering the nature of this "closet" disorder, physicians should be vigilant in questioning patients, so that the possibility of anxiety or panic disorder is actually considered—if the symptoms are there. Truth is, few people plagued by these problems will try to get help. Many are afraid that when they voice hard-to-articulate concerns, their doctors' eyes will glaze over, the same way their friends act when the problem is mentioned. It is very helpful for a patient to tell a doctor about any anxiety-related symptoms.

Even though it's hard to admit in an "enlightened" society, Americans still harbor some long-held beliefs that mental problems are embarrassing, at the least. And, some who suffer from anxiety and panic attacks decide to withdraw from society rather than seek help.

Clearly, the toll that anxiety and panic attacks can take is absolutely amazing, and this fact has become increasingly evident to those in the business of healthcare. As many as half of patients with recurrent chest pain and normal coronary arteries don't have heart problems—they have panic disorder.

Chest pains are among the most problematic of anxiety symptoms, in that these often send people to the emergency room. Recurrent chest pains in the presence of normal coronary arteries is a common and perplexing problem in primary care medicine and cardiology, resulting in significant healthcare utilization. A series of carefully controlled studies in the past decade have suggested a strong association between this syndrome and the presence of anxiety disorders. A high percentage (30 to 50) of patients with recurrent chest pain and normal coronary arteries meet existing criteria for panic disorder. Generalized anxiety disorder is also associated with this syndrome.

Drugs that slam-dunk panic

Panic disorder is a biological illness, with real symptoms. It is widely believed that the causes of panic attacks are biological and psychosocial. So, for many people, it takes both psychological treatment and medication to treat this problem. Usually, panic attacks don't just disappear spontaneously.

Prescription drugs used to reduce the symptoms of panic attacks and other anxiety disorders include: selective serotonin reuptake inhibitors (SSRIs), beta-blockers, benzodiazepines, tricyclic antidepressants, phenothiazines, and other medicines, such as BuSpar and Effexor XR.

Researchers believe that panic attacks are associated with neurotransmitter problems—in particular, those involving serotonin, norepinephrine, and dopamine. Long-term drug therapy may be necessary to correct your chemical imbalance. Your physician will monitor your response, and the pharmacologic therapy may be changed, to determine if another medication, or a combination of them, works better. If your doctor takes you off medication after extended treatment, you may have a recurrence of symptoms after you taper off, which may require another startup of drug therapy— or may indicate the need for long-term maintenance therapy.

Thanks to their effectiveness in treating anxiety and depression, the SSRIs have become some of the most widely used drugs in the world. They are believed to increase the amount of serotonin available to the brain. Some of these include Prozac (fluoxetine), Zoloft (sertraline), Paxil (paroxetine), Celexa (citalopram), and Luvox (fluvoxamine). Paxil is probably the most ballyhooed of drugs for social anxiety disorder.

SSRIs are widely accepted as the first line of treatment because of their effectiveness and the low incidence of serious side effects. For example, Paxil usually results in fewer, less intense panic attacks. Further, the patient experiences less depression and less anxiety in general in most cases. Initial dosing is usually low, and the dosage is raised gradually.

Benzodiazepines often prescribed for acute anxiety and panic disorders include: Xanax (alprazolam), Klonopin (clonazepam), Ativan (lorazepam), Tranxene (clorazepate), Valium (diazepam), and Librium (chlordiazepoxide). These are usually considered best for short-term use only. Many health experts believe that the best benzodiazepines for treating panic disorder are Xanax and Klonopin because they go to work quickly and have side effects that are usually tolerated well. On the other hand, if the sufferer has a history of alcohol or substance abuse, benzodiazepines are not a good choice. A major downside of this class of drugs is the possibility of physiological dependence. When these are withdrawn, some patients do fine, while others have trouble with relapse of anxiety symptoms, withdrawal, or rebound problems.

Some benzodiazepines that are often referred to as sleeping pills are: Halcion (triazolam), Dalmane (flurazepam), and Restoril (temazepam). These, used on a short-term basis, work well for severe

acute anxiety. However, they are used infrequently because continued use results in tolerance, which makes increased dosages necessary, thus putting the patient at risk for a greater incidence of side
effects (lethargy, fatigue) and withdrawal problems (insomnia, anxiety) when the drug is discontinued.

Monoamine oxidase inhibitors (MAOIs) treat panic disorder
effectively, but they can have severe adverse effects, especially
through interaction with a number of other substances (sympatho-
mimetics, dopaminergics, foods containing tyramine, SSRIs,
Demerol, the cough medicine dextromethorphan)—so they are best
reserved for patients who fail to get relief from other drugs.

MAOIs affect the brain's neurotransmitters called the monoam-
ines: serotonin, norepinephrine, and dopamine. The MAOIs block
the action of the enzyme *monoamine oxidase*, thus leaving more of
these substances for the brain. Research tells us that MAOIs such
as Nardil (phenelzine) effectively reduce social anxiety symptoms.
But, as mentioned before, these strong medicines are not the first
line of attack because they do not combine well with certain medications and foods; in fact, they can cause severe elevations in blood
pressure. MAOIs are also associated with weight gain.

Drugs that are also used to treat panic attacks are: BuSpar
(buspirone), Serzone (nefazodone), Effexor (venlafaxine), and
Remeron (mirtazapine). Panic sufferers who have been unresponsive
to other medications are usually prescribed beta-blockers; clonidine;
calcium channel blockers; antipsychotics; or anticonvulsants, such as
Depakote (divalproex) and Neurontin (gabapentin).

In patients who have both depression and anxiety, antidepressants
(such as the SSRIs and tricyclic antidepressants) are effective. They
also work well for panic attacks and mood swings. However, before
the drug begins to take hold, there can be a dicey period of depression
that on rare occasions torques into suicidal tendencies. After about
three weeks, most anxious and depressed patients enter into an
elevated mood state, with an increased sense of well-being. Common
tricyclic antidepressant medications are: Elavil (amitriptyline),
Sinequan (doxepin), Norpramin (desipramine), and Tofranil (imi-
pramine). These drugs elevate the levels of certain neurotransmitters
in the brain, specifically, the ones that regulate mood and personality.

Individual suitability to each antidepressant is highly variable, which means that a patient often must try several (sequentially, not at once) to pin down the one that is most effective. Some side effects associated with medications for anxiety and depression include: nausea, drowsiness, dry mouth, constipation, impotence, and agitation.

Among medical students, "stage fright" drugs called beta-blockers are popular for single-dose use prior to oral exams or presentations. Inderal (propranolol) and Tenormin (atenolol) target problems of anxiety such as rapid heart rate and trembling. They reduce nervous system hyperactivity by blocking transmission of nerve impulses to the beta-type receptors of the sympathetic nervous system. Beta-blockers are used commonly for anxiety symptoms, such as heart palpitations, and they slow down the heart rate. (Beta-blockers are most commonly used in the treatment of high blood pressure, and are also prophylaxis against migraine headaches.)

Undoubtedly, drugs can be effective in reducing anxiety, but drug studies often show a major down side: a high relapse rate if medication is discontinued early. And in most cases, the only way that stopping a medication does not result in a setback is when there is also psychotherapeutic intervention.

Naysayers on drug intervention also cite the controversy over the relationship between suicidal behavior and fluoxetine (Prozac) use. A report given in the *Journal of Clinical Psychiatry* (April 1996) examines the relationship between fluoxetine use and suicidal behavior in the Harvard/Brown Anxiety Disorders Research Program (HARP). Probabilities of suicidal behavior for 654 subjects were examined. Those patients not using fluoxetine during follow-up had almost twice the probability of making a suicide attempt or gesture than subjects on the drug. Those having episodes of major depressive disorder at intake were more likely than those not having an episode to receive fluoxetine during follow-up.

Rethinking fears, putting on anxiety-buster gloves

In controlled trials, the only psychotherapy that has been shown effective against anxiety disorders is cognitive-behavioral. Psychiatrists report great success in helping anxious people "talk through" their anxiety-evoking situations. Cognitive therapy definitely can help someone see a problem differently simply by the exercise of reframing it.

Panic patients—often rather anxious people to start with—benefit from being taught the difference between normal emotions and anxiety. Behavioral therapy calls for exposure to anxiety-provoking stimuli in gradually greater exposures, which can desensitize you to the experience over a period of time. Cognitive therapy involves learning to understand false beliefs and distortions and gaining an understanding of panic attacks. You learn what the physical sensations are, master ways of controlling anxiety, and understand what things can trigger attacks. You learn that you won't die during a panic attack.

What seems to work best on panic disorder is combining the two approaches—cognitive-behavioral therapy and medication. Most people improve dramatically in a matter of weeks.

To learn to cope, be patient and have realistic expectations. Although some people do get better quickly, others see slow progress. Setbacks are almost a given. To improve your life while you're working on eliminating panic attacks, try to reduce your number of obligations and don't take on new duties or assignments. Improve your diet and exercise regimens and get more rest, with an emphasis on regular bedtimes.

You will soon find ways to view your panic situations differently. You will slant your attention in another direction, or become desensitized to the fearful situation by exposing yourself to gradual "mind video-clips" of the situations you've avoided. Then, when you face the real situations, you will feel like your skills are strong enough to manage attacks.

Behavioral therapy helps many anxiety sufferers to resume fully functional lives. If you don't have access to anyone trained in behavioral therapies, you can probably benefit from a do-it-yourself repertoire, combining regular exercise, stress-reduction and relaxation techniques, and self-help literature. (You must avoid recreational drug use and alcohol consumption because these substances can impact the course of panic disorder, and thus, interfere with your goal of eliminating or curbing panic attacks.)

What can happen if you don't seek treatment?

Sometimes, people who fail to seek treatment spiral lower and lower. Their lives deteriorate and even holding down a job becomes difficult.

Both personally and professionally, the panic-attack sufferer may fail to thrive. Some experts believe that about half of panic-disorder patients are likely to be financially dependent on someone else. Major depression is often a troubling problem, and some people end up self-medicating, which can lead to drug addiction.

Panic disorder can be disabling, and sometimes gives birth to phobias that can restrict life, such as agoraphobia (fear of public places). Furthermore, the rate of suicide attempts in those with panic disorder is very high. If you do have panic attacks repeatedly, **seek treatment**.

You feel overwhelming anxiety, but no panic attacks...yet

What happens if you're filled with anxiety much of the time, but you're not having panic attacks? You've read what they are like, and that's not what happens to you.

You may have a condition spawned by excessive anxiety, such as generalized anxiety disorder, post-traumatic stress disorder, obsessive-compulsive disorder, or phobic disorder. These are the psychiatric disorders found most commonly in the United States, but, amazingly, it is estimated that up to one-half of patients with anxiety disorders aren't diagnosed accurately. This failure to diagnose correctly and appropriately treat anxiety disorders results in overuse of healthcare services and increased disease and death rates from either the anxiety disorder or from spin-off medical conditions.

To confuse matters further, consider the fact that panic disorder is often seen in combination with mood swings, substance abuse disorders, and other anxiety disorders. Those who experience panic attacks often relapse, and may experience panic attacks for many years. Also, to show what a quirky beast a panic attack can be, some people have a single episode and then never experience another!

Can you conquer anxiety in a fast-paced, high-tech world?

Sometimes, we want to blame the world for our anxiety. But in fact, people aren't really terribly different from the way they were in our ancestors' time. However, society *has* changed massively. Unfortunately, we haven't grown much wiser in dealing with the huge changes that have come down the pike one after another. Technology alone is enough to terrify techno-duds. If you're not up-to-date with the latest computers, PDAs, and devices, you may doubt your ability to be an asset in today's workplace.

We're also ravaged by the grim results of several decades of divorced parents and disintegrating family values. Teens are meaner to their peers. Adults are more backbiting and aggressive in the workplace. Parents get out of sync with their children because adulthood often feels like a stress-filled crucible where they're imprisoned. When you were a little girl playing with your Barbies, or a little boy with Tonka trucks and G.I. Joe, this was not what you expected your life to be like, right?

So, I can sit with you and discuss your anxiety all day long. Or I can talk to you about "issues" and how to give yourself permission to be happy. But what good is that when what you really need are tools, answers, and plenty of tender loving care?

To make sure I was on the right track, I asked the most anxiety-ridden woman I know (someone facing possible imprisonment because of a brush with the IRS). Marcy* listed three things she needed to help keep her anxiety to a level that was tolerable and not debilitating:

- Friends who would support her and give her reassurance that her life wasn't over.
- A way to enjoy her days despite the nightmare her life had become.
- Tools for handling and reducing the symptoms of her depression and her panic attacks, which include shortness of breath and a pounding heart.

How did your life get so screwed up?

In one respect, you're probably like my friend Marcy—you just want to be happy. You want, somehow, to finesse your way into some beautiful, dreamy place where you'll find someone special, and your life will be peaceful and fun and harmonious...and your heart won't have to beat 90 miles an hour all the time because you're so wrought up.

But wait a minute, you say—*not so fast there*. This mess is only to be expected because things went *way* wrong. You married the wrong person. Or you chose the wrong career. Or you've lived for years in a hailstorm of stress and demands. And now, you're so wired that breathing in and out has become difficult. How did you get yourself in such a mess? And more important, how can you get out?

Well, you don't have to "diagnose" how you got here. I know how frustrated you feel—and I also know how to lead you out of the quagmire. Having suffered anxiety and panic, I've gained a certain level of "panic smarts." I can get you to a better state, where you will be around people who will lift you up, and you'll know exactly what to do when panic seizes you. You'll have a clear vision of what it takes to make your life happier—and how to get just that. You'll redefine your reality and come out smiling, by reaching deep within to call on greater internal resources than you ever knew you had. The saucy new you will have no reason to panic anymore.

No longer are you going to be kept down under the thumb of past bad breaks, low self-image, others' naysaying, or cloudy future prospects. You're going to push the "clear" button on your life, and start anew. And we'll get you set up to succeed. Think of it, essentially, as a pilgrimage to find your essence: what unravels you; what you fear and why; what you want and how to get it; and what forces in your life are holding you back.

Then, we'll work on rewiring you so that, in as little as 30 days, you can learn to enjoy panic-free living that's happier than anything you ever imagined possible. You'll never again hear yourself saying "you know how I hate social situations," or "you know me—I always self-destruct." You can benefit tremendously from the combination of your doctor's professional medical attention, the help of a psychotherapist, and your brand-new attitude changes, all of which will mesh well and lead to an improved quality of life.

• • •

So, right this very minute, stop saying that the deck has been stacked against you. Look to the day you're living in—and tomorrow. Past mistakes won't run by again so that you can fix them, no matter how much you'd like a second shot at grabbing that brass ring. That never happens.

One reason life holds so much promise is that you can change anything today—if you try—and if you can figure out how to do it. Obviously, you're tired of feeling fearful or you wouldn't be reading this book. What we'll do is provide you with the tools for a miraculous self-saving. You will truly hop in there and rescue yourself.

Wait. Oh, no. I hear you wimping out already. You're coming up with excuses: "But, listen, Dr. Shoquist, you have no idea what I have to cope with! I'm stuck with an awful husband, four lazy kids, a dead-end job, relatives who borrow money, and on top of that, I'm constipated!"

No excuse exists that is valid enough to take you off the hook. If you can articulate the words "I want a happier life that is free of panic," then you can do exactly that, no matter what your burdens and drawbacks.

How bad is it?

To kick off our anxiety-busting project, let's find out exactly how bad off you are. You're committed enough to admit, so far, that your life could use some improvement, and having to deal with anxiety makes daily life more difficult. But, can you really let down your hair, shake off the constraints of being conventional, and try some new and different things?

Discover if you're really up for self-reinventing—one of the facets of our anxiety-busting plan—by answering the following questions:

1. If we ask you to sketch a rough picture of your family, would you try?
2. Are you willing to examine yourself—good and bad points—and be honest enough to entertain the notion of making changes?
3. Would you sample new approaches if it meant memorizing a game plan?
4. Can you imagine yourself becoming a bit different— perhaps happy and satisfied instead of being a nail-biting neurotic?
5. Can you stop the habit of "donating" positive traits to people you know in order to make them not seem so objectionable? Can you walk away from these negative folks if necessary?
6. Would you attempt to pinpoint your wacky behaviors, name them, and try to work on shedding them if they're holding you back?
7. Would you try some suggestions for getting outside of yourself to help people in need?
8. Will you go through a step-by-step growth plan intended to get rid of panic attacks and bring you more peace?
9. Can you make more time for enjoying sensory pleasures: smells, tastes, music, physicality?
10. Are you willing to shake up things a bit—alter your current habits and venture into some exotic realms and practices?

Sound too scary? Answering yes to all of the above may shake you far from your comfort zone. But, trying new things will take you in a new direction and help you shrug off that old excuse of "I've always been like that." Just listen to the grimness of those words! It's as if you're saying that you have always been fairly worthless, or unhappy, or ineffective. How sad that sounds!

And, if you do define yourself in negative terms, why not try a new way of thinking: Look at the heavens, throw your head back, thrust out your arms, and reach for the stars just to see what happens. You have nothing to lose but time. On the bright side, the incredible payoff if the plan succeeds is that proverbial pot-of-gold at the end of the rainbow. We don't mean money when we talk about gold—we mean self-satisfaction, peacefulness, and happiness like you've never known before. (And who knows, maybe money will come with it, too!)

How do I know for sure that I need help for anxiety?

Many signals can tip the scales, pointing up disastrous levels of anxiety. So, if you feel like anxiety and panic are disabling you, check out your status by answering the following questions:

- Do you think people are always evaluating you and discovering that your performances fall short?
- Do you hesitate to move forward and take action because someone might criticize what you do?
- Do you have such great fears of certain situations that you avoid them altogether if you can?
- Do you find yourself often feeling anxious?
- Do you have serious doubts about your abilities, your intelligence, and your appearance (self-esteem issues)?
- Do certain situations cause you to feel panicky?
- Do you let phobias back you into a corner?
- Do you have many fears?
- Are you jittery and nervous?
- Is it almost impossible for you to make decisions?
- Do you feel tightly wound up?

If four or more of these fit your profile, you definitely have anxiety. And, you may have the most common kind of anxiety—social anxiety disorder—which means you obsess about performing poorly and looking bad. You're afraid that people around you are studying what you're doing and you dread being scrutinized. More than anything, you have a huge fear that your behavior—on the job, at a party, on a date—will embarrass you.

You can shake the grip of panic

No matter how far gone you are, you still have time to get better. Don't even worry if self-defeating thought processes are so built in that you're already sure our plan won't work for you.

It doesn't matter what has happened to you in the past, or how many times you've tried to eliminate your demons, only to fail. Even if you're miserable to the point of feeling dejected, hurt, and sad beyond belief, you can give this thing another chance by simply repeating our cheesy little one-line mantra: "I'd like to believe I can stop having panic attacks and live a happier life."

Just say that. Give us a few hours of your time.

Understanding children's anxiety

Watch your children closely. Social anxiety disorder usually has an early onset and shows up most often during adolescence. Because children and adolescents usually don't complain about their anxiety symptoms, and/or because these symptoms are often not brought to the attention of a doctor, the most typical scenario is that treatment is delayed until much later in life, when a person finally receives therapy for something else, such as panic attacks.

Children who are especially at risk are those who showed marked anxiety when they were left with outside caregivers because their mothers had jobs. Separation anxiety disorder in childhood often bears a link to adult cases of anxiety disorder.

Stressful life events frequently increase anxiety, leading to the development of full-blown disorders. As reported in *Archives of General Psychiatry,* in a study of parent-adolescent disagreements in 303 families with an adolescent (12 or 13 years old), researchers found that many children internalized their anxiety symptoms. They didn't talk about their troubles, but didn't deal with them effectively, either. The anxiety created an emotional "hole." By age 19 or 20, when these subjects were assessed for anxiety and depressive disorders, evidence showed that stressors, such as disagreements with parents, caused them to hone their habit of internalizing conflict. They would suppress awful feelings and hope they would go away. That didn't work, so their anxiety problems, left untreated, just got worse.

Parents with social phobia seem to role-model this problem for their kids. The observation that genetics and environment are joint launching pads for anxiety is proven by studies. For example, when researchers looked at 1,047 adolescents ages 14 to 17 (*Archives of General Psychiatry,* September 2000), they saw a strong association between parental social phobia and social phobia in offspring.

Also, parents who had other psychological problems had adolescent offspring with social phobia. If the parents suffer from depression, anxiety disorder, and alcoholism, their children often experience difficulty with wanting to go places, do things, and form friendships. Parents who are overprotective and ones who reject their children often have children who develop social phobia.

Seniors and fears

At the other end of the age spectrum, the elderly have their own anxiety problems that are caused by their life situation and/or pathological causes. Pathologic anxiety may even disable a previously high-functioning older adult. In late life, anxiety symptoms include impaired concentration and attention, impaired memory, dizziness, disabling fear, severe insomnia, and hyper-vigilance, among others. Clearly, proper treatment is desperately needed.

Many times, though, seniors' anxiety symptoms are confused with more severe disorders—dementia, delirium, depression, and even psychosis.

Strong data now link coronary artery disease (CAD) with depression, anxiety, personality factors and character traits, social isolation, and chronic life stress, with an especially strong link in the cases of depression and social isolation, according to *Patient Care* (August 1999). Plus, researchers think that anxiety, depression, and social isolation may have negative effects on neuroendocrine or platelet function. Heart-diet guru Dean Ornish, M.D., says that toxic emotions can even contribute to constricting your arteries, and he advises addressing the mind/body/spirit connection with a few minutes of meditation each day.

Honing anxiety-busting skills

No doubt about it, anxiety is a major problem in our society, affecting everyone from kids to seniors. But, what actually works to make things better is debated. Important findings come from a study documented in the *Journal of Anxiety Disorders* (September 2000), in which researchers focused on determining whether group social-skills training or group behavior modification was more effective in treating social anxiety. These findings supported the growing belief that practically nothing works better than teaching those afflicted *how* to cope better. The patients who received social-skills training showed a *significantly greater reduction of social anxiety and a greater increase in social skills* than the other group. At follow-up, the social anxiety and social-skills scores of those who received social-skills training, actually reached normal levels, whereas the other participants improved only to the point of nonsocially anxious patients with anxiety disorders.

This means that people can learn to curb anxiety by developing and using coping skills. Learn how to use the following (described in Chapter 3), and you'll find a few that feel like a good fit for you:

- Assertiveness training.
- Defusing demons by sorting beliefs.
- Positive self-talk.
- Changing responses to cues (reframing).
- Improving social skills.
- Fine-tuning relationship-building.
- Anger management.
- Learning to avoid blame-shifting.
- Effective expression of needs.
- Bolstering with nurturing and compassion.
- Thought-stopping.
- Role-playing and visualization.
- Inoculating against stressors.
- Nutrition enhancement.
- Exercise regimen.

The bottom line is...

Remember that anxiety and fear are not synonyms. With fear, you know what you are frightened by. Anxiety is an amorphous, wispy dread that sneaks up and grabs you.

In a time when high-tech innovations can make anyone feel out of step overnight, it's a good idea to reassess how you're living and decide if it's really necessary for you to wear three beepers, spend hours on a cell phone, and be conversant in the latest Internet jargon. Perhaps, you would be better off at times to watch mindless TV (cartoons are good), relax with your family, or try a new craft or hobby on weekends.

Learn to say no. Take a break to socialize. Don't think that you have to spend every waking hour fine-tuning your multitasking, and working to be the brightest of the bright.

If you know that what you're experiencing is many notches above normal stress and anxiety, find a way to have a better life. *No More Panic Attacks* is packed with ideas on ways to ease your anxiety-burden and ratchet up your hardiness for facing fears. Anxiety-busting can be a true adventure—if you're willing to change existing behaviors that really aren't working for you.

2

Take the 2002 Life Quality Test

FOR MANY YEARS, A POPULAR TOOL TO ASSESS LEVELS OF STRESS was the Holmes-Rahe Stress Scale, first published in 1967 (Holmes, T.H. and Rahe, R.H. The social readjustment rating scale. *Journal of Psychosomatic Research*, Vol. II). Essentially, what makes a life occurrence stressful is that you're required to make adjustments when your normal routine has been altered.

The Holmes-Rahe Scale assigned a "stress rating" for various life events experienced in the previous year. A high figure indicated that you were overstressed, based on the assumption that you tolerated stress well.

But, one flaw in using this 35-year-old scale today is that it doesn't take into account new stressors of the Information Age. And, the premise of the 1967 scale is that all forms of change are stressful, whether these are desirable events (such as marriage) or undesirable events (such as a tax audit). But such a scale cannot weigh an individual's exact perception of an event. Clearly, your own perception is what makes an event stressful for you—or not. This raises the question: How can you discover your own rating when perceptions of events differ so greatly?

Another variable is how an event affects an individual at different times in life. A change in financial status probably devastates a retired 75-year-old, while a young attorney may take a layoff in stride. Furthermore, the issues that plague Baby Boomers (failing health, pressure to stay looking young, loneliness) must be weighed. No doubt, a correlation exists between illness and stressful events, although *many people who live frenzied lives do not become ill.*

Because many people researching stress today have found the old stress rating scale dated, some have done knock-offs. For example, the Internet has a Student Stress Scale, as well as one tailored to women.

So, the authors of *No More Panic Attacks* bring you a new 2002 Life Quality Test for adults—one that fits today's concerns and problems.

Here's how it works

To determine your stress level, assign a value, *depending on the strength of the impact on you*, to each of these "stressors" that you experienced in the past year. For an ongoing problem that you obsessed about, attach a score of 100 to 200. A stressor that troubled you some of the time gets 50 to 99. Give the others 10 to 49, ranging from a frequent stressor (49) to an occasional stressor (10). Add up your score and then go to step two.

Because we all have life factors that "soften" the stress in our lives, in step two, subtract points *based on the good things that are going on.*

Step 1

- ☐ **Anxiety-maker #1:** You experienced death of a mate or parent, or a catastrophic event.
- ☐ **Anxiety-maker #2:** You experienced separation and/or divorce.
- ☐ **Anxiety-maker #3:** You're stressed by threat of jail or incarceration.

☐ **Anxiety-maker #4:** You are facing drug addiction in self or mate.

☐ **Anxiety-maker #5:** You experienced reversal of fortune, foreclosure, repossession.

☐ **Anxiety-maker #6:** You got fired, laid off, or expelled from school.

☐ **Anxiety-maker #7:** You're dealing with rape or unwanted pregnancy.

☐ **Anxiety-maker #8:** You're facing cancer or other serious illness in self, mate, or relative.

☐ **Anxiety-maker #9:** You are experiencing sexual dysfunction.

☐ **Anxiety-maker #10:** You are stressed by long-term job boredom or overload.

☐ **Anxiety-maker #11:** You're experiencing domestic abuse (physical).

☐ **Anxiety-maker #12:** You are stressed by having your parents living with you.

☐ **Anxiety-maker #13:** You feel anxiety because your child, parent, or sibling is getting a divorce.

☐ **Anxiety-maker #14:** You're experiencing a traumatic workplace betrayal.

☐ **Anxiety-maker #15:** You feel anxious because your live-in lover won't marry you.

☐ **Anxiety-maker #16:** You are anxious because your mate is addicted to the Internet.

☐ **Anxiety-maker #17:** You're going through chemotherapy.

☐ **Anxiety-maker #18:** You're having appearance and dieting anxiety.

☐ **Anxiety-maker #19:** You feel anxious because your mate cheated on you.

☐ **Anxiety-maker #20:** You feel panicky when your child curses and smart-mouths you.

☐ **Anxiety-maker #21:** You obsess about your inability to find work and pay bills.

☐ **Anxiety-maker #22:** You worry about lacking computer savvy.

☐ **Anxiety-maker #23:** You're stressed because the IRS is pursuing you.

☐ **Anxiety-maker #24:** You're stressed by planning a wedding or another big event.

☐ **Anxiety-maker #25:** You have an eating disorder.

☐ **Anxiety-maker #26:** Your coworkers are difficult to deal with.

☐ **Anxiety-maker #27:** Single-parenting issues cause you anxiety.

☐ **Anxiety-maker #28:** You're bothered by inconsiderate antics of grown kids.

☐ **Anxiety-maker #29:** You're stressed by the development of a lifelong STD (herpes or HIV).

☐ **Anxiety-maker #30:** You have concerns about your child taking drugs.

☐ **Anxiety-maker #31:** Your son or daughter left home for college or marriage.

☐ **Anxiety-maker #32:** You experience strong fears of social situations.

☐ **Anxiety-maker #33:** You are having in vitro fertilization, but you worry that nothing will work.

☐ **Anxiety-maker #34:** You gave birth and had fears relating to rearing a child.

☐ **Anxiety-maker #35:** You became a stepparent.

☐ **Anxiety-maker #36:** You experienced stress because your work responsibilities have increased or changed.

☐ **Anxiety-maker #37:** You feel anxiety related to being a three-beeper high achiever.

☐ **Anxiety-maker #38:** Your mate demands to get married.

☐ **Anxiety-maker #39:** You worry about your shyness and innate inadequacies.

- ☐ **Anxiety-maker #40:** Your grown offspring has a destructive relationship.
- ☐ **Anxiety-maker #41:** An interfering in-law erodes your peace of mind.
- ☐ **Anxiety-maker #42:** An ex-spouse gives you and your kids grief.
- ☐ **Anxiety-maker #43:** You're feeling stressed by your spouse's bad temper.
- ☐ **Anxiety-maker #44:** You worry about your ticking biological clock.
- ☐ **Anxiety-maker #45:** You moved.
- ☐ **Anxiety-maker #46:** Your mate stopped working (loss of second income).
- ☐ **Anxiety-maker #47:** You felt financial worries and/or depression at the holidays.
- ☐ **Anxiety-maker #48:** A mean boss causes you anxiety.
- ☐ **Anxiety-maker #49:** You obsess about old grievances and grudges.
- ☐ **Anxiety-maker #50:** You're experiencing litigation stress.
- ☐ **Anxiety-maker #51:** You're conflicted about staying with your current mate.
- ☐ **Anxiety-maker #52:** You started school or had other change in responsibilities.
- ☐ **Anxiety-maker #53:** You're experiencing anxiety over sexual performance.
- ☐ **Anxiety-maker #54:** You worry about being a bore and you fear rejection.
- ☐ **Anxiety-maker #55:** You experienced job-review or job-interview stress.
- ☐ **Anxiety-maker #56:** You are starting menopause.
- ☐ **Anxiety-maker #57:** You experience bouts of fear concerning public speaking.
- ☐ **Anxiety-maker #58:** You feel extreme concerns about aging.

☐ **Anxiety-maker #59:** You feel financial distress, with no hope in sight.

☐ **Anxiety-maker #60:** You worry about your employees' opinions of you as supervisor.

☐ **Anxiety-maker #61:** You feel terribly anxious when people drive erratically.

☐ **Anxiety-maker #62:** Your fears are causing compulsive behaviors.

☐ **Anxiety-maker #63:** You had a traffic accident or minor law violation.

☐ **Anxiety-maker #64:** You obsess about your inability to get housework done.

☐ **Anxiety-maker #65:** You hate your job.

☐ **Anxiety-maker #66:** You're stressed because you're an unloving, critical parent but you don't know how to change.

☐ **Anxiety-maker #67:** You worry about your mate's shopping addiction.

☐ **Anxiety-maker #68:** You're bothered by your mate's constant, obnoxious nagging.

☐ **Anxiety-maker #69:** You feel anxiety because your baby cries often.

☐ **Anxiety-maker #70:** You worry about your inability to meet spouse's expectations.

☐ **Anxiety-maker #71:** You obsess about an inherited gene for cancer.

☐ **Anxiety-maker #72:** Your decreased vision and hearing make you anxious.

☐ **Anxiety-maker #73:** You feel anxious because your beloved pet died.

☐ **Anxiety-maker #74:** You worry about your teen's casual attitude toward sexual activity.

☐ **Anxiety-maker #75:** You experience anxiety over stressful conversations.

☐ **Anxiety-maker #76:** You worry about workplace violence.

☐ **Anxiety-maker #77:** You obsess about your child's safety at school.

☐ **Anxiety-maker #78:** You worry about violence in the world today.

☐ **Anxiety-maker #79:** You obsess about personal safety precautions.

☐ **Anxiety-maker #80:** You are afraid to drive a car.

☐ **Anxiety-maker #81:** You're stressed because people owe you money.

☐ **Anxiety-maker #82:** You're stressed because someone close to you frequently hurts your feelings.

☐ **Anxiety-maker #83:** You obsess about your marriage ending in divorce.

☐ **Anxiety-maker #84:** You feel great anxiety from being in a tempestuous relationship.

☐ **Anxiety-maker #85:** You feel anxious about your stock-market losses.

☐ **Anxiety-maker #86:** You're stressed by loss of money in a failed business venture.

☐ **Anxiety-maker #87:** You worry about retirement funds being insufficient.

☐ **Anxiety-maker #88:** You feel anxious because you're a new retiree or new graduate.

☐ **Anxiety-maker #89:** You feel anxiety over a family member's mental illness.

☐ **Anxiety-maker #90:** You worry constantly about your child's chronic illness or disability.

☐ **Anxiety-maker #91:** You feel anxiety about your child's developmental problems.

☐ **Anxiety-maker #92:** You experience anxiety over your inability to save money.

☐ **Anxiety-maker #93:** You worry about your inability to get a large amount of work done.

- ☐ **Anxiety-maker #94:** A supervisor or teacher makes demands that cause you to feel panicky.
- ☐ **Anxiety-maker #95:** You fear you have failed as a parent.
- ☐ **Anxiety-maker #96:** You worry that your mate is showing signs of growing discontent.
- ☐ **Anxiety-maker #97:** Your fear of flying makes you unable to travel.
- ☐ **Anxiety-maker #98:** You're plagued by worries about floods, fires, and other natural disasters.
- ☐ **Anxiety-maker #99:** You feel anxious about your child's cruelty to animals.
- ☐ **Anxiety-maker #100:** Your mate demeans you and rarely says a kind word, but you're too anxious and depressed to leave.

Step 2

Now, alter your tally by applying the softening effect that comes from the pluses in your life. For the mitigating factors listed below, subtract points:

- ☐ **100 points:** You have a happy marriage/relationship with someone you love.
- ☐ **100 points:** You have a child (young or grown) who is a source of happiness.
- ☐ **75 points:** You have no child or parent living in the household (and this excludes negative scenarios, such as a child you're estranged from, a runaway, a parent placed in nursing home against his will, and so forth.)
- ☐ **75 points:** You have a positive workplace situation—you feel in control of your fate and often receive positive feedback.
- ☐ **75 points:** You have sufficient cash flow for a comfortable lifestyle.
- ☐ **75 points:** You have a spiritual outlet that is satisfying and peace-giving.
- ☐ **50 points:** You have an entertaining and relaxing pet.

☐ **50 points:** You have a harmonious relationship with extended family.

☐ **50 points:** You have positive and reinforcing friendships.

☐ **50 points:** You have accomplished a lifetime goal.

☐ **40 points:** You participate in a stress-relieving hobby, sport, or other activity.

☐ **40 points:** You participate in volunteer work or charity work.

Tallying your score

Look at your final tally, and read on, to see how that translates into Your Personal Anxiety Level:

If you scored 600 to 1,200 or more, you should seek help in dealing with anxiety and panic. This level of stress can be a real detriment to your health and possibly lead to dysfunction and disease.

If you scored 300 to 599, your anxiety level may be high enough to hurt your health. Try some of the coping skills (Chapter 3) to curb your responses to stress, and consider seeing a doctor.

A score of 100 to 299 means you probably can benefit from learning a few stress-curbing tactics.

Less than 99, and you can call yourself a member of the "hardy personality" group. Stress tends to roll right off your back. Good for you!

If you pulled off a minus score, you must be reading this book to find ways to help friends and relatives. Obviously, *you know how to handle anxiety.* In Chapters 5 through 11, we look at 100 scenarios involving all of the anxiety-provoking situations listed here.

3

Gearing Up for Success:
Your Anxiety-Busting Skills

IMAGINE HAVING THE ABILITY TO KNOW WITH TOTAL CERTAINTY THAT you can be happy and have a satisfying life—and quit worrying! No matter what fate throws you—bad health, lawsuits, business failure, loss of employment, divorce, betrayal, abandonment—you'll draw on your hardy personality traits and keep repeating, *"I won't let forces outside of me prevent a good life. I'll maintain an attitude that is free of malice and negativity. I believe in myself and my ability to cope with change and disappointment and joy."*

And in your quest to develop a flexible and indomitable hardy personality, you don't need to worry that you'll end up hard as nails. You'll still keep your core softness and compassion, but add to the mix some handy skills that will help you weather storms unscathed. If what you've been doing hasn't worked, you have little to lose by changing your approach—and everything to gain.

Assertiveness training

Some people have a hard time believing they *really* have rights, and they certainly don't stand up for them. Others who lack assertiveness actually know they have rights—but no role model or mentor has ever shown them an effective, nonabrasive way of exerting themselves.

For example, let's look at a situation that you find irritating: Your spouse refuses to let you know when he is running late. When you bring it up, your concerns are blown off with an "oh well, that's me" attitude—cavalier and infuriating.

The assertive way of dealing with this would be to decide in advance what you plan to say so that you don't fly by the seat of your pants, with nonproductive threats and name-calling. What you will do is express what's bothering you about what your spouse is doing, how you feel about it, how it impacts your life, and what you would like to see done differently. Try this, for example: "I feel upset when you don't call to let me know you're running late. I often have dinner ready, and I'm left sitting here with the kids, not knowing whether to start without you, or wait for you. I would love to get a phone call from you saying 'I'll be about an hour late because I'm going to run by the gym and do a quick workout' or whatever. Please work with me here."

Your attitude should be serious, not whining or pitiful. Skew your language and voice to make it clear that you expect a response because you know he or she cares what you think.

However, let's assume that you get a negative response. Your spouse barks back this: "Hey, I won't let you boss me around. I'll come home late when I want to and I'm not going to let you henpeck me into calling first. Forget about it. Get off my back!"

What comes next? You simply restate what you said before, firmly and calmly. Don't slink away. Stay assertive, and pleasant, and positive. What you're asking for is perfectly reasonable and fair; you decided that before you decided to put it on the table. So, have no qualms about it. Be strong.

If your spouse persists (bullheaded and unbending), set up a tone that says that you want to work this out. However, have a second line of offense scripted in advance. Take this example: "I can see that you feel strongly about not having to answer to me, but I also believe you care about inconveniencing the kids and me. I think it would be common courtesy to call, so how about just giving it a try, to see if it works to help us have smoother lives? It would be respectful, and I think that's something we pledged to each other when we got married. I try to respect your needs and requests."

If your spouse agrees to try it once, thank him for listening to you. This is very important and doesn't come under the heading of "kissing up" to someone. Say that you really appreciate his willingness to give this a shot and that it means a lot to you.

Give kisses and hugs. Show that working together is a positive thing, not a mean-spirited standoff. You're not trying to win. You just want some considerate treatment.

Even if you found the response less than loving, you still need to give thanks for the slightest smidge of cooperation. Remember, results are what you're looking for. How you get there doesn't matter in the long run. When your spouse actually follows through and gives you a call, give an honest "thank you."

If your spouse continues to fail to deliver what you agreed upon, reiterate: "I hope you'll remember to give me that call we agreed on, the next time you're running late." There is no need for shouting, name-calling, or recriminations. Just pummel him with patience and positive expectations, and you will get good results from even the most stubborn human being on earth. Try this method with children, mates, bosses, coworkers, or in-laws.

Here are the steps to assertiveness:

1. Remind yourself that you have rights. You have a right to expect your mate to be interested in meeting your needs, just like you're concerned with meeting his or hers.
2. Decide what you plan to say when asking for changes in a situation that is disturbing you.
3. Vow that you won't use name-calling, threats, old hurts, or tired scenarios of things that have disappointed you in the past.
4. Have a talk, when you both have some uninterrupted time. Set up a meeting time and day.
5. Say what's bothering you, how you feel about it, how it impacts your life, and what changes you are looking for—what you would like to have your mate, child, or employee do differently.

6. Keep your attitude upbeat, optimistic, and workable.

7. Don't whine or act pitiful.

8. Show that you fully expect a good response because you know that person cares what you think.

9. If the other person reacts in a defensive or uncooperative way, restate your desire for change, and be firm and serious—but not icy.

10. Keep your voice positive and pleasant.

11. If necessary, go to your secondary script: "I can see you don't want to make this change, so I'll just thank you for listening to what I've said—and ask you to give it some thought, please."

12. If the person agrees to "try," give thanks—mate, employee, coworker, child, or parent. Say something that expresses your sincere happiness at this person's willingness to listen and agreement to try.

13. Go your separate ways (to work, the gym, or to feed the kids). Try to make a point of finding something totally unrelated that you can commend the "problem-person" on at some moment during the same day. The message is this: We're people who care about each other, and we appreciate and respect each other, so we need to work together to solve problems.

Defusing demons by sorting beliefs

Everyone has fears. Some are *rational*—things we should be afraid of if we have good sense. Others are *irrational*—things that logic tells us we should not fear but logic seems to be saying this in some foreign language that is unintelligible.

To defuse your fears, sort your thoughts into two stacks: rational and irrational. First, list things you're scared of that are logical: world catastrophes, fire, gunfire, plane crashes, car wrecks, and so forth. Then, list the monster that gives rise to panic (For example, "I fear that I am going to lose my job because I have a sneaking suspicion I'm not very good at it. And that feels awful.")

The road to defusing a fear goes like this:

Clarify what the disturbing thought is

You've already done that in the previous section.

Look for concrete signs that this is true

How fully do you believe this statement? Give yourself three points for each of the following if your answer to the question is *yes*:

- Do other people in the workplace tell you that your work isn't good enough?
- Has your supervisor ever indicated that you might get fired?
- Has any support person in your life (husband, grown child, best friend) ever suggested that you should change jobs because you're not good at what you do?

If you come up with a total of nine points, you're probably looking at a fear that is grounded in reality. That means you can get rid of your anxiety by finding something that's a better fit for your skills. If you have no specific work skills, decide what kind of training you could seek that would lead you to another profession.

But, what if your score was six or three? You've gotten negative feedback—but you haven't been declared a washout. Your fears appear to be *somewhat* grounded in reality. Find a way to improve your performance or find another job that's a more natural line of work for you.

A third scenario could be that you're just a big worrywart who imagines the worst from the scantest of evidence.

Whatever your level of trepidation, the following are ways to defuse your demons by sorting beliefs:

Turn things around and try to imagine the point of view of your boss and your coworkers

Be as realistic as you can. If your supervisor could tell you one thing about your work that needs improvement, what would it be? Perhaps you need to be more creative in your projects, more punctual, or more organized. If you sense that you know your flaw, vow to improve. Then ask yourself if you were in your supervisor's place, would you fire someone who had the assets you have: good worker, comes to work every day, has a cheerful attitude, and gets work in on time?

You'd probably keep that person, and ask her to work on her shortcomings. Wouldn't that be easier than finding and training a new employee, and then having to work with that person's drawbacks?

You're faced with the worst outcome, and you know how to deal with it

Now, presume that the worst does happen. Your supervisor wants cutbacks or doesn't want to give you time to find a way to improve, so he fires you.

According to your monster theories, you suspected that if the worst did happen, you would die or go nuts or mutate into a four-headed demon. None of these is the outcome. You've already anticipated the third step, and you've also decided how you would deal with it. Tackle it by saying you would simply find another job. Your script: "I won't act like this is the worst thing that has ever happened in the world. It's a disappointment, but I can handle disappointments because I have done so in the past."

Think through your "demons"; decide what your options are

When you find yourself hand-wringing, quickly move on to problem-solving. Decide what you'd like to be doing in one year, and realize that by that point, this will be far behind you, and hopefully, you'll have a job you like better and that you feel you're good at.

With a plan sketched out, do something for yourself. Take a walk or go to the gym. Let your mind wander. And count your blessings—you're a healthy enough person, in mind and body, to be able to look for a job.

Finally, move into action mode

Begin sending out resumes, or get on the Internet and check out job sites. Talk to friends about jobs, and ask those close to you what they think your strengths are.

If you're not sure what you want to do, go to a state or community facility that offers aptitude tests. You may find a career you didn't even know existed.

• • •

To sum up, here are the steps in defusing demons by sorting beliefs:

- Take your fear out to examine it.
- Sort your thoughts into two stacks: rational and irrational.
- Look for specific signs that your scary thought is actually true. ("If I'm in my car today, I'll undoubtedly get carjacked.") Can you say that you're sure this will happen? No, of course, you can't. Call it what it is—an irrational fear.
- Give your fear a rating (1 to 10) as to how grounded in reality it is.
- Think of ways you can make your "fear" less likely to become a reality. If you have a fear of being carjacked, you can be alert, take along your cell phone, and refuse to stop for people who urge you to pull over to the side of the road.
- Then, think of what you'll do if the worst does happen. Will you die, or will you just hand over your car and collect insurance money?
- Do what you can to kill this "monster" in your mind. Think it through. Know what your options are.

Positive self-talk

One of the easiest, handiest coping skills is "self-talk." It can have absolutely amazing power. Self-affirming statements get you through stressful times and remind you of what's important—having a good life, contributing to society, and staying a positive force in others' lives.

Sure, affirmations get mocked on *Saturday Night Live*—Al Franken as the character Stuart Smalley, looking in the mirror and chanting, "I'm good enough, I'm smart enough, and, gosh darn it, people like me." But the reality is, self-talk really does work, and thousands of people rely on affirmations to get them through tough times.

Pare down your current self-talk to get rid of all negative messages. If you monitor your self-talk for one day, you'll be shocked how many nonproductive thoughts dance through your mind.

Look at 49-year-old Celia*. Celia's husband divorced her a year ago. Full of self-doubt and 15 pounds overweight, she feels out of the loop in a youth-oriented culture. She's very anxious when she goes to the gym, has a date, and even when she's doing things with friends.

Here is the list of negative thoughts that she needs to shed:

1. People in the gym and in restaurants are looking at me and thinking "What's that old bag doing in here?"
2. Any man who goes out with me will think he's on a date with a loser. I've been divorced twice, I have no idea what to wear on dates, and I need to lose 15 pounds.
3. No one will want me because I'm so filled with stress and anxiety that I'm not even a good conversationalist anymore. I am a dud.
4. My parents always told me that I needed to work on my shyness, and learn to be a better talker…and they were right—I'm bad at those things.

Look at each piece of self-talk. Is it helpful? Is it true? Probably not. She should consider the following:

1. How do you know people in the gym are judging you? Rewrite your thought: "They're looking at me simply because people like to look at other people. Anyone who judges people with a negative comment wouldn't be anyone I'd want to know anyway."
2. On aging, think this: "I've had my time to be 20 and 30, and now is my time to be older. The same thing happens to everyone."
3. If a man is taking you out, he wants your friendship or companionship or wants to know you better. Take the sting out of the whole thing with this thought: "I want to see if we can be friends. I can always use another friend, and apparently, he can, too. If it turns into something more than that, it would be nice, but it's not necessary."

4. As for your weight and clothes, if those things bother you, get some help from professionals. Hire a personal trainer for a results-oriented exercise program. If you can't afford a trainer, start a regular walking program or join a gym, along with improving your diet.

    Also, find a personal shopper or a salesperson in a fashionable boutique and ask for advice on what "works."

5. The divorce topic requires revising your thoughts. This isn't always a deal-killer—many people are divorced, and you'll probably date some of them. They aren't likely to judge you for marriages that didn't work out.

6. Accept that you're experiencing anxiety, but turn this in a good direction: "I accept that I feel nervous and anxious, and that isn't unusual, considering how long it has been since I've been on a first date. To cope with my anxious feelings, I'll focus my attention on my date, on making him feel accepted." If you can focus on his interesting qualities, you'll lose all self-consciousness. Turning a date into a "friendship opportunity" is such a win-win situation that it simply can't backfire. Either you wind up with a new friend or a new date, or both.

7. *So what* if your parents told you that you needed work? They weren't right about everything, and maybe they were wrong about that. Try the radical idea of saying: "I'm all right the way I am."

One mother tells of having a very shy 7-year-old daughter who was happy and had a small circle of friends. A brash neighbor told the mom one day, "You really need to do something about Jill's shyness—she'll never get anywhere like that." The girl's mother believed in building on her daughter's strengths and letting her develop in her own way. Gradually, as Jill gained a foothold in school, she became an academic standout. Because she was still shy, she had to learn to cope with situations that terrified her, such as speaking in front of the class. Her mother helped her on a per-situation basis. The bottom line: Jill did not have to revamp her personality. She finished college with honors; completed medical school and a residency; and became a doctor, wife, and mother. She's still shy, but she's also a wonderful listener, an excellent diagnostician, and a favorite of friends and coworkers for her sincerity, warmth, and fun-loving nature. Not everyone has to be outgoing.

• • •

Recapping, here are the steps of self-talk:

1. Get rid of negative thoughts you constantly tell yourself. Eliminate thoughts such as, "I'll never get anywhere in this job because people hate me." When something like this floats into your mind, send it away.

2. Replace each negative with a positive. "I'll reach my goals in my profession because I'm willing to devote time and energy and a strong work ethic to my job."

Changing responses to cues (reframing)

Think of the saying "don't beat a dead horse." Look at that image. This should be enough to carry you through to action with your nagging thoughts. You need to change your responses to certain cues in order to alleviate your anxiety. Just because you've always interpreted a particular comment in a certain way doesn't mean you can't "reframe" that idea. For example, if your supervisor tells you that you need to take more initiative, your knee-jerk response may be this: "What does he know? He just hates me, and besides, I'm doing everything I can to take charge in my work."

To reframe this situation, think about taking a look at your supervisor's pointer. Maybe you do need to take more initiative. Brainstorm about ways you could respond. Make some concrete moves to take initiative in the workplace in new and different ways. Get rid of the "he hates me" reaction; maybe he's just being straightforward and expressing expectations, which he has every right to do as your supervisor. Turn the subject over and over, and you'll be able to sample ways to change your responses to cues.

A man named Brent* learned how to use reframing. He was having difficulty with entrepreneurship because part of the job involved wining and dining. He hated long dinners and felt inept in social situations. He told his business partner, "That's just how I am. Why should I change? I'll never be effective at parties."

However, his business partner was tired of shouldering the entire responsibility of schmoozing clients, along with all her other responsibilities. She wanted some support in socializing; and if he couldn't give it, she was ready to end the partnership.

That announcement was enough to make Brent consider changing. Can I become someone different at age 40? Could I handle the anxiety of trying to make it through a social evening? Enduring a cocktail party sounded like having his throat slit. He had strong fears of social functions. This is what he told himself:

- My parents never taught me anything. I'm too screwed up to do well in cocktail-party situations. They failed to help me thrive socially.
- I don't see my dismal performances in social situations changing.
- I'm anxiety-ridden because my social skills—or lack thereof—are messing up my business.

So first, he needed greater awareness of the possibility for change. If you hear yourself repeatedly responding to cues with, "I can't change—that's just me," take a look at your negativity. Ask yourself:

1. Am I positive that this is a trait that cannot be improved?
2. Am I positive that there is no help for my social anxiety?

As an enlightened businessman, he knew the answers. No, he wasn't sure that he was a hopeless case. No, he hadn't checked into getting help.

Pushed into a corner, Brent reviewed his stand on the matter. Looking at the way he liked to blame his parents, he realized this was a crutch. He hated that kind of rationalization. He often told his friends, "Hey, get over it." His parents had tried to rear him properly, but now that he was grown, this was his problem—not theirs.

He tackled the second negative thought: "I'm ineffective in social situations and I don't see that changing." The first part was true, but the second was off. He knew that people could change things about themselves they didn't like—he had given up drugs when he was 24. Wouldn't this be easy compared to shaking substance abuse?

The last problem—anxiety because this was eroding at his business success—well, that one was fixed once he acquired social skills. In preparation, Brent began to give different responses to his partner's cues. He told her: "I'll improve. Give me some time."

• • •

Here are two steps in changing responses to cues:

1. Come up with a new way to look at an old stressor. Take this example: Your mate never gives you a "real" compliment—just generic ones such as "you always look good." This has always bugged you, but now you're "reframing" it. In its new perspective, you see the words for what they are— a natural response from a person who's reserved and not very expressive. Think of all the qualities your mate has that you love, and ask yourself if trading your mate for one who's more effusive with compliments would be worth it (what if you end up with a flatterer who's a cheater or a drug addict?). Decide not to be so sensitive to your mate's blanket gestures.

2. Tackle negative thoughts by using this technique. Let old cues inspire new responses that reflect your newly hardy personality. You're in charge of your life, and you're nobody's victim.

Improving social skills

Most people who want to improve social skills are looking for instant gratification, although achieving significant change is usually a gradual process. As in the case of Brent whose partner had tired of carrying the social load of their company, there can be a reason that some changes must be implemented as soon as possible. In other cases, an individual may want to change without any rush, and can take a leisurely approach to self-improvement.

Brent, believing he had no time to take a course or read a book, turned to the most socially skilled person he knew—his partner. He asked her how he should approach this problem. She told him that early in life she had learned two keys to social success: Concentrate on people (make eye contact, smile at them, listen carefully to them) and ask questions about their lives (find out if they have hobbies, sports they like, children, aspirations, and so forth). She uncovered things in a casual way, but usually walked away from interactions with all kinds of information about the person she was with.

His response was typical: "But I don't want to know anything about other people, so why should I ask?"

Again, he needed to remember why he was asking these questions. He claimed he wanted to "get better," which would call for tweaking himself into a more outgoing, more other-centered person.

He had some idea of what to say and do, but how would he get rid of preconceived notions about himself? This called for reframing or revising his responses to cues. Ordinarily, when he went to a cocktail party or was seated at a four-hour wine-tasting dinner, he let his mind rerun specific negative thoughts that made him mute and sullen. The new idea was to try "thought-stopping." His partner suggested that when he began to think of himself as a know-nothing social loser, he could replace the thought with something more optimistic, like that he was a continental dude exploring the world. That made him laugh, at least.

He described the thoughts that usually ran through his head at parties: "Why would anyone want to talk to me? They're judging me. I have nothing to say to these people."

His partner gave him some thoughts for using during socially anxious moments:

- "Everyone who's here wants to talk to someone, so why not me?"

- "No one is judging me any more than I'm judging them. They're just out for an evening and want to have a good time."

- "I will have things to say to these people—I'll ask about their interests. If that topic dries up, I'll tell them a few things about my work—the only thing I can really cut loose on."

Incidentally, Brent's first time out, this worked for him. His partner went along just to help him feel safe, but he was able to talk and be somewhat "entertaining." He concentrated on helping others have a good time. As time went by, he felt less dread about social situations, although he never really loved them.

• • •

Try the following to improve your social skills:

1. Study the things a socially skilled person does.
2. Concentrate on people you talk to, make eye contact, smile, and listen carefully.
3. Ask questions about their lives.
4. Think of yourself as a brand-new "social animal."
5. Remember that other people are more interested in what you think of them than they are in evaluating you and your party skills.

Fine-tuning relationship-building

Following are some ways to enhance your ability in building good relationships:

Look for opportunities to spend time with the person you want to get to know

Whether you're fine-tuning a bond with a relative, a client, or a friend, if you don't show up, you can't improve a relationship.

Tuck away your self-absorption as you walk out the door

You have polished your appearance (clothes, hair, makeup, and so forth), so you're making a conscious choice to leave behind any preoccupation with how you look, stand, twitch—whatever.

When you talk and listen, try to develop a "flow" to the conversation

You need to resist the very human impulse to line up what you want to say while the other person is talking. Stop planning your next words and listen with every neuron in you. Listen fully. Believe us when we say that the person you are talking to is happier to know he or she is being heard than hearing you share.

Expect to feel exhilarated by the exchange of information

Show acceptance by giving your full focus and enthusiasm—the person you're with will love this. Think of people you've known whom everyone flocked around. What is the common denominator? Genuine interest in others. What matters is how that person feels when he's with you.

While your initial stabs at this may feel a bit "fake" and difficult because you're forcing them, don't let that trip you up. You'll discover that truly concentrating on another person is very satisfying. Naturally, it makes that person seek you out. And that's a good feeling.

When you get home or back to the office, make notes of things you want to remember about the person you were with

These could be the name of his son, the fact that he likes to sail, his fleet of miniature schnauzers, the trip he has planned, his wife's name—anything. Many people put this info in their computer address book, along with address/phone number/e-mail address. That way, when you contact this person, you'll have something personal to talk about: the latest feat of his wrestling-champ son, that trip to Maui, or the dog show. But don't overdo it. Every single time you call, don't ask the same thing over and over as if you're following a script.

• • •

Use these tips for relationship-building:

1. Forget yourself so you can focus on others.
2. When someone talks, fully engage that person (don't be planning your next comment so that you're only half-listening).
3. Show enthusiasm for the conversation.
4. Try to remember some important things about the person you talked to: his children's names, her favorite sport, among others.

Anger management

You may feel anxious because you know you have a tendency to blow up and lose your temper. This isn't a good thing, and you know it. However, handling your anger hasn't improved, despite your awareness of the drawback it is. You have frequent road rage, you explode at coworkers and family—you are a walking powder keg.

Maurizio Fava, M.D., and Jerrold F. Rosenbaum, M.D., have researched "anger attacks." They found that often, these mimic the symptoms of panic attacks but happen without fear or anxiety—and usually occur when a person has been arguing with his mate and goes ballistic in a way that is out of proportion to the particular situation.

Is your anger cranking up your level of anxiety? To find out, designate the following statements true or false to discover if your anger is inappropriate and over-the-top enough to point to a need for treatment:

- I get angry quite often.
- Frequently, my anger is extremely intense.
- I get angry in situations in which I can't afford to come unglued.
- My anger sometimes leads to aggressive, unleashed behavior that causes me problems.
- Small things can make me explode in anger.

If you answered true to even one or two of these, this is something you need to work on. Because coping with anger is a gigantic issue, for the purposes of this book, we can only hit the high points of anger management. The first of these is facing the truth—that your anger is a problem. Next, you work on noticing the chain of events that leads to an outburst of anger.

Let's presume that you are lashing out at your mate often, and that person tells you that it comes from nowhere, and thinks the level of anger is unwarranted. A mood spiral is often behind an outburst of anger. Are you sometimes angry with yourself? Bored? Just feeling impatient and agitated?

Try to identify that "last straw" that begins the trigger. Maybe you explode every time your spouse asks you to do something and you happen to be feeling moody. You're mad that you're being rushed, even if your mate isn't rushing you. Try to break down the interaction, and decide if you could be overreacting to the amount of pressure being applied. Is the pressure coming from within you?

Factors that influence your "patience IQ" are your genetics, your personality, and your tolerance level (this comes from childhood experiences). Typical negatives in people who have hot tempers are somewhat subconscious thoughts such as:

- "I'll lash out when I notice that someone is pushing me."
- "I'll dig in my heels rather than respond to what I perceive as a demand."
- "I hate having people demand quick action of me when I'm otherwise occupied."
- "I don't think you're treating me like I deserve to be treated."

If you recognize any of these as your triggers, be honest with yourself about your rigidity. "If that person in the next car doesn't move quickly when the light changes to green, I'll honk at him. I won't give him five seconds." Could you adjust your expectations? When the driver in front of you doesn't move as quickly as you would like, think something like:

- "He's obviously not in a big hurry."
- "That could be my 80-year-old mother behind the wheel."
- "I could be five minutes late, but everyone knows the traffic here is unpredictable."

In other words, revise your hot buttons; don't just assume that you're correct in thinking that it's your duty to get all the drivers on the road in line. You're not the driving-infractions police, so get over yourself. *Lighten up.*

Anger-management steps are as follows:

1. Accept that you feel angry sometimes, and try to identify the situations that make you blow up—and what events precipitated the anger.
2. Come up with lines to repeat or actions to go through when you feel your anger at a rolling boil. For example: "I need to relax and put this in perspective. I need to think before acting or saying something I may regret."

3. Ask yourself if it's smart to take the situation so seriously. Visualize your hands taking the knots inside your stomach and slowly unwinding them, relaxing the tension that's causing you anxiety. Imagine a soothing massage, and your body gradually relaxing into a looser, less taut state.

4. Consider taking a different approach when the same situation comes up again. For example, your mate asks you to put a new toner cartridge in the printer, which has, in the past, upset you ("I'm always being pressured to do something right that minute"). But is that what really happened or what you imagined? Repeat this: "I'm just being asked to replace the toner. It doesn't have to be done right now. I'm not being asked to rewrite the Constitution. I'm the one blowing this out of proportion, so this is my problem."

You're indulging in distorted thinking, and difficult as it is, you need to try to make yourself admit this and work on it. Many people distort situations. Examine this and tone down your overreactions.

As we mentioned before, anger management is complex. If you have this problem, you need to seek further help—join an anger management group, see a psychologist, do something to help yourself.

Learning to avoid blame-shifting

This classic skill can help you bust anxiety in many situations. When you find your anxiety welling up because of things "other people are doing," look at what's really happening. Usually, you want to blame another person rather than taking responsibility for your own actions.

Case in point: Susannah* goes out for an evening of dining and dancing that turns sour when she gets a little bit drunk. She begins to make a spectacle of herself on the dance floor, doing a crazy erotic dance that simulates stripping. No one else is out on the dance floor. All eyes are on her. Her husband cringes; there's a tangible chill between them when she returns to the table. As they leave the club, she lashes out at him: "It's all your fault because you were no fun. Why do you have to act like that?"

He points out that things were just fine until she got drunk and began her bump-and-grind, which turned him off. But she kept shifting the blame back to him, refusing to believe that she had done anything wrong.

This is common couple trouble because it's so hard for us to see ourselves as other people see us. If you have a standoff, try hard to look at the situation from the other person's point of view and search for a shred of truth in what he or she is saying. Usually, you will find it.

You can decrease your own anxiety in couple communication by accepting that blame-shifting is human...but not productive. You'll never increase the intimacy in your relationship by refusing to take responsibility for your less-than-terrific actions. You probably hate finding out that you're not perfect—but it's really all right.

Also, Susannah's acceptance of some responsibility for the evening falling apart will be very endearing to her mate. On the other hand, her clinging to the belief that it was "all his fault" is rigid, and gets them nowhere as a couple. Most misunderstandings involve at least two people, right? And, typically, both are imperfect.

You can learn to avoid blame-shifting by doing the following:

1. When someone gives you words of criticism (constructive or otherwise), consider the comments carefully before firing back.
2. Think before you speak. It's easy to lash out when someone makes you feel uncomfortable or angry by pointing out your shortcomings.
3. Consider the possibility that the person may actually have a point.
4. When you respond, do so in a way that's self-preserving, but positive and nonjudgmental.

Effective expression of needs

Many divorces have resulted from one partner's inability to read the other's mind. This sounds silly, of course, but think how many times you see one person sitting around, wishing that her husband knew her needs...but failing to express them clearly. Who is the one off track here? Whether it's mother-child, sister-brother, husband-wife, you must give up the idea of mind-reading if you want to have a truly close relationship with someone else.

A woman complains, "I feel anxiety all the time because my father doesn't appreciate living in my home."

• • •

She should use the following steps in effective need-expression:

1. Ask yourself what you would like for him to do differently. Fold clothes? Run errands? Express verbal thanks? Not interfere in your child-rearing efforts or marriage?

2. Try saying what you need to hear from him, or what actions you want to see happen. You shouldn't expect your father automatically to know what you want. Perhaps, he would be perfectly willing to deliver if you were better at expressing your desires. If it's impossible for you to say what you want, write down your thoughts and hand the piece of paper to him. Don't be rude or hateful; just be specific and talk about how the situation makes you feel.

3. Express appreciation for his cooperation or willingness to consider what you've asked.

4. Express your love every chance you get.

Bolstering with nurturing and compassion

To decrease your anxiety, get outside of your preoccupation with yourself ("I have such a dismal, dreary life—woe is me!"). Improve your life by extending yourself and reaching out. Whether you nurture a puppy, a child, or a friend, you'll find that the movement toward another decreases your own worries.

Think of ways to show compassion when you wake up each morning. What can I do today that will make my husband feel loved? How can I help my child feel good about herself? Can I make my coworkers feel acknowledged and cared for? Can I work toward using fewer negatives in my talks with people and more positive comments?

No matter what your source of anxiety—impending deposition, financial worries, new in-laws—you can achieve a higher plane of consciousness by taking some sort of "other-oriented" move. Why waste time crying in your beer when you can be a positive force in someone else's life?

• • •

Here are steps in bolstering:

1. For people in your inner circle, find things you can do to make their days better.
2. For strangers in need of help, think of ways you can make their lives better.
3. Make living compassionately one of your top priorities.

Thought-stopping

One of the very best anxiety-handling techniques is thought-stopping. "Whoa. Wait. I'm not taking my thoughts in that direction."

Not so easy, you say? Try the following tips for ways you can curb your anxiety by halting erroneous or negative thoughts:

Imagine yourself in the situation that scares you

Case in point: Dave* visualizes himself in the situation that evokes strong fears. He's in an elevator in his office building, and suddenly feels like he's suffocating. Thoughts of being in an elevator in the doomed World Trade Center on September 11th overwhelm Dave. He has to get out; he feels his heart pounding and he's breathless.

Give yourself the "stop" signal

He tells himself "stop" when he first gets caught up in the negative thought and the fear signals start.

He says "stop!"

The next day he imagines himself at the same place, but this time instead of singing out the word, he whispers it. "Stop," he tells himself.

Say it in your mind

In his mind, he tells himself, "stop."

Test your thought-stopping

He gets into an elevator. When the fearful thoughts rush him, he forgets what he's supposed to do. He tells himself not to entertain gruesome ideas. That works. In the elevator, he starts to think about what could happen, but he sends the thoughts away with a firm "no" that comes from his mind.

Do another test-check of your stopping word

The next day he tackles saying no when he feels his head swirling with thoughts of being caught in the elevator. This time, the thought is powerful and he feels good about its success. He presses his fingers on his temples when he tells himself "no" to reinforce the message.

The spiral still occurs when he's in elevators, but now he has a coping mechanism to control his anxiety. The "cure" isn't an over-night success, but it gradually gains force as the skill becomes natural to him. To his "stopping word," he added some self-talk: "I know I probably won't suffocate or die in an elevator. I'll be all right and I'll soon be getting off the elevator to get on with my day."

• • •

To reiterate, here are the steps in thought-stopping:

1. Imagine yourself in the situation you fear, and think of telling yourself to stop the chain of thoughts that lead to panic.
2. Picture a stop sign you can flash in your mind, or actually make one on an index card to carry in your pocket.
3. Test your thought-stopping technique.
4. Practice stopping negative and unproductive thoughts.

Role-playing and visualization

Role-playing is great for decreasing anxiety, especially in children.

A 5-year-old at a homeless shelter had fears about starting school. He was not bonded with any adult (like a mom or dad). As a volunteer at the shelter, I was playing games with little Leo* the week before the start of school. I asked him, "Would you like for me to tell you what it will be like on your first day of school?"

He immediately dropped the toys he was playing with and said "yes," and came over closer so I could fill him in. I told him we would "pretend" I was his teacher. I told him about lining up, and he marched into place. I told him about raising his hand to ask a question, and Leo practiced that. And I reassured him that his cheerful attitude and big smile were things that his new teacher would really enjoy about him. We talked about things they would do and how he could benefit from listening carefully. He seemed more relaxed and comforted.

• • •

The steps in visualization are as follows:

1. Think of the situation you're worried about, and imagine yourself walking toward it.
2. Imagine yourself going through the situation in a confident, unafraid manner. You're striding past the fear and making the situation a good experience.
3. Do this until you feel comfortable with the idea of seeing yourself in the feared scenario—but handling it with flair and confidence, like a pro.

Inoculating against stressors

The hardy individual inoculates herself with many traits:

- This person is convinced that she has control of her destiny.
- The hardy individual works toward certain goals, and maintains specific priorities, and it's hard to drag that person from that path.
- The hardy individual seeks challenges and figures out how to meet these, handling all sorts of stress-jolts in the process.
- This person uses coping skills that work.
- The hardy individual has commitments that are important—personal, family, career, and fun.

- On a case-by-case basis, everything is handled calmly and deliberately. Aided by a higher power, the empowered individual controls destiny.

For example, Ellie* is caught in gridlock, and people all around her are losing their tempers. Much like others smelling the exhaust fumes floating by, she feels her heart rate speed up, her neck feels stiff, her mouth is dry. But unlike many of those stuck on the freeway, she knows where to go. Thinking of her Sun Scene—a special place on the beach, in the sun—she lets her mind fly off so that when she glances at the driver in the next car, who's also stuck in the freeway mess, she can smile and nod, as if to say "we'll make it through this—it's just a little snag."

Then, after the wreck is cleared off, someone from the back of the pack of cars comes zooming past, certain that his mission is more important than any other driver's. Ellie wishes him well in his frenzied existence and even manages a positive thought: "I'm glad I don't obsess over losing 30 minutes stuck on the freeway to the point that it makes me arrogant."

• • •

Here are the steps you can use in inoculating yourself against stressors:

1. Remind yourself of your new approach: You're in control of your destiny. You work toward your specific goals and passions. You have priorities, and no one can pull you off that path, or decrease your enthusiasm for it.
2. Review your coping skills.
3. Keep in mind your important commitments.
4. Handle stressors calmly and deliberately.
5. Imagine giving yourself an "injection" or shot against something that has previously hobbled you. Now, you're set to go—it can't touch you!

Nutrition enhancement

One thing you can do to reduce your stress load is fuel up in a good way.

Studies prove that certain foods should be avoided by those who are plagued with anxiety (which would be most of the population in the United States). Examples include: mood-affecting substances, such as salt, sugar, alcohol, and caffeinated beverages (including carbonated drinks, coffee, and tea). Avoid eating too much fatty, high-cholesterol food, which clogs arteries and can make you fat. And avoid chocolate, which makes your blood sugar spike, allowing you to feel better temporarily, but making you feel worse when it goes back down.

Smart foods to choose are ones that are high in fiber (whole-grain breads and cereals, beans, peas, whole-grain pastas). Fruits and vegetables are good. Berries are excellent. Dark foods (breads, pasta, veggies) are better than light and white ones. Don't overdo your meat intake.

Eating the right foods can help you cope better with stress. Much research links anxiety and other mood disorders to neurotransmitters (molecules that carry messages from one brain cell over to another). To that end, remember to get enough of the B vitamins daily. Vitamin B is believed to help regulate serotonin, dopamine, and norepinephrine, which are three key neurotransmitters. Because high doses of B-vitamin supplements can be toxic, get your B quota from greens, tuna, beef liver, salmon, asparagus, pork chops, sunflower seeds, grains, kidney beans. (And don't forget a daily multivitamin.)

Aim for 1 to 2 grams daily of omega-3s, which serve to keep your spirits high. Saltwater fish, such as salmon, albacore tuna, and mackerel have lots of omega-3s— essential fatty acids that help maintain your nerve cells and balance dopamine and serotonin. Heart guru Dean Ornish says you should take fish-oil supplements daily to help you ward off heart disease.

Another good anxiety-reducer is selenium—get about 55 micrograms daily. But don't go overboard—no more than 400 micrograms a day. Good sources include beef liver, tuna, halibut, salmon, chicken breast, oatmeal, whole-wheat bread, Brazil nuts, lean beef, and raw oysters.

Watch out for diets that ask you to eliminate or curb carbs, which tend to reduce the production of serotonin, a lack of which can cause mood swings, depression, and agitation. You'll feel more in control with a daily serotonin boost from carbs—about 300 grams a day is fine. Good sources include bananas, apples, whole-wheat pasta, baked potato, whole-wheat bagels, oatmeal, cranberry juice.

Exercise regimen

Adding exercise to your life may help you to a spectacular degree. If it improves your health alone, that's enough to make it worth doing. But in many cases, people definitely find exercise a vital part of reducing anxiety.

Here are two key tips: Find something you like, and make sure it's convenient. If you don't like the workout, you'll find it easy to abandon when the new wears off. And if the gym you join isn't close to your home or work, you'll start making excuses not to go.

And what about home-exercise equipment? For most people, these pieces end up gathering dust and building guilt. The majority of exercisers stay more faithful to their programs when they go somewhere and do something. That can be taking to the street each morning for a three-mile walk. That can mean doing weight-training at a nearby gym. It can be a dance class, martial-arts training, fun runs, or any of an assortment of options for getting and staying fit.

Exercise is a fine way to unwind and release stress. It's also good for making you feel that you're doing something for yourself, to stay healthy, to look your best, to maintain your weight. When walking, you can clear your mind, plan your day, say your prayers, make mental lists—and generally feel vibrant. Chances are good that, during cool-down, you'll feel calmer and more in charge of your fate.

Because excessive anxiety means you're probably rather tense, you should embark on a new exercise program slowly. Do something simple, such as taking a walk. Put the pedal to the metal after you get used to having exercise as a part of your week.

• • •

So, what's your best bet? That depends on your goals, but here are a few approaches:

- Work out for anxiety reduction and general health. Do some form of aerobic exercise and weight-training. At home, you can exercise with free weights, and walk briskly four days a week. Or join a gym and get a fitness consultant to set up your machine/weight workout and lead you through it, illustrating correct form and execution.

- Aim for weight loss and body-toning. To take off weight, you need to increase your amount of movement, and that means at least three days a week of exercise: Spinning, bench classes, dancing, running, walking, basketball, and so forth. Hire a personal trainer to set up the bodysculpting aspect of your training program; ask the manager of a health club for the names of trainers who know how to help you get results. Every training program features certain standard elements for full-body improvement, but each individual has different goals and problems.

Let's roll!

None of us will ever forget the heroic words of Todd Beamer, who died on the ill-fated flight that was intended to wipe out one more American landmark on September 11, 2001, but was stopped by a group of courageous passengers who decided they simply would not let another atrocity happen.

Use your highest level of resolve to decide that you're going to get in charge of your life, and you're going to refuse to let anxiety make the rules. Choose your favorite anxiety-busting skills, improve your eating and exercise regimens, and go forward with joyful optimism.

Your fears have been holding you back, but you're about to turn that into ancient history. A new you is in the pipeline, and you're putting on the finishing touches!

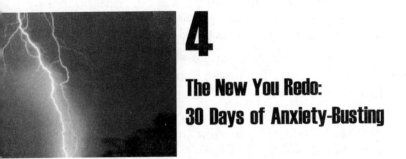

4

The New You Redo:
30 Days of Anxiety-Busting

BY FOLLOWING THE GUIDELINES HERE, IN 30 DAYS OR LESS, YOU MAY be able to eliminate your panic attacks entirely by dealing with anxiety-causing situations in new ways. At the end of this process, you'll be the poster child for hardy-personality traits.

Why? Having a "hardy personality" makes you less suscep-tible to illnesses spawned by stressful events. And studies sup-port the theory that developing a set of hardiness-oriented skills can serve as a permanent fix for your anxiety woes. Using the advantages of a strengthening approach, you can stress-proof your personality.

And, while you may not be invincible, you'll definitely be far better at curbing anxiety than you are now. Even for someone who's just battling everyday "stress," these skills can help to settle anx-iousness and ease emotional discomfort.

Get your doctor's take on the problem

Of course, you *must* see your physician first if panic attacks or anxiety is scaring you or causing you to drop out of life—or if you feel like you may be depressed. Before you go in for your appointment, jot down the symptoms that you've been having so that you can effectively describe what you have experienced.

To get a feel for what a panic sufferer goes through, imagine what it was like being on the 100th floor of the World Trade Center, suddenly surrounded by balls of fire. You panic: your heart pounds wildly, your body trembles. Now, imagine that you're having these same symptoms but there's no disaster: you're just sitting in a class or at your desk at work. You try to compute why you're feeling such bizarre things, and you think, "I'm losing it completely! This has to be a heart attack!"

The fact is, having a fight-or-flight reaction to things that scare you is perfectly normal. Coping with life-threatening situations causes physical responses such as adrenaline release, fast breathing, and sweating. But, if you feel these things when there's no legitimate danger, that's probably a panic attack (assuming it's not a heart attack). Despite the scariness of the symptoms, you really won't die or go insane, no matter how sure you are that something awful is happening. (However, if this is your first panic attack, you need to be evaluated by a physician to make sure there's not a medical cause for your symptoms.)

So, what causes such horrible panic? Some people have a genetic propensity for panic attacks, while others are at greater risk when they're overtired, overstressed, and underexercised. Perhaps, a certain situation just makes you feel threatened, whether or not that perception is accurate—and that combines with a buildup of stress. The result: You react with an *overreaction*. Your body freaks. You think you're going crazy or having a heart attack. You thrash around, looking for a way out of your predicament.

Unfortunately, the individual who has experienced this kind of terror begins to monitor his or her life perpetually, always expecting a reappearance of the symptoms. This leads to increased anxiousness and exaggerated vigilance. Many people will totally avoid situations that they associate with the first panic attack. This underscores how very important it is to examine your fear and find a way to conquer it.

To diagnose your problem, your doctor will take a medical history and perform a thorough medical examination in order to rule out other reasons that you may be having these symptoms. Many medical conditions mimic the symptoms of panic/anxiety disorders, so you shouldn't skip the medical step.

If your physician does conclude that you have a panic or anxiety disorder, the next moves are: understanding the panic spiral, and figuring out what you can do about it.

Understand how fear leads to panic symptoms

Here's the typical rundown of a panic attack: You confront (or expect to confront) a situation that you fear (such as a snake, a cliff, rising water, or crowds). Or, you have an out-of-the-blue attack of intense fear with impending doom. Symptoms come on quickly and peak within minutes; your heart pounds (heart rate is increased), and you are sweating and having chills, shortness of breath, trembling, and dizziness. You wonder if you're losing your mind, or having a heart attack. Try to expose yourself to these symptoms in your mind, or in reality, and observe the outcome: You didn't die. You didn't go crazy. You lived.

Some people need a therapist to lead them through pinpointing the earliest feelings in the pattern that grows into panic, and help bolster them in changing responses. Others prefer to hunt and pillage themselves, and oftentimes, can carry it out quite effectively.

But, you must find a way to target erroneous thoughts such as "I'm probably having a heart attack" or "I feel like I'm dying," and replace those with more logical thoughts: "I'm feeling odd, but it will go away soon." This helps to reduce your anxiety level.

During Week One of the 30-day plan, you'll learn to manage a panic attack...and discover how great that feels.

Can you really alter your behavior?

Absolutely. You can learn a new habit in as little as 30 days.

You may want to use all or parts of the plan, and see what works best for you. Spend a month going through the steps, and then keep the parts you like and weed out those that don't suit you.

Remember, simply avoiding situations that terrify you is nothing but a short-term solution. Your anxiety will increase with each exposure until you address the cause. Don't let this mess up your life! Understand your fear, and fine-tune your plan that will help you cope effectively.

The 30-day plan: Week One

Think of an individual you've known or observed who is confident, at peace with herself, and in control of her actions. Now, try to learn to approach life the way your "model" does—fearlessly and proactively. In psychobabble (the official language of psychiatrists), you're "participant modeling" when you imitate a hardy personality.

What follows is the rundown for the first week of our 30-day plan:

Start each day with a hardy-personality psych-up time (during your shower, breakfast, or morning exercise)

Try this sample script for self-talk:

"I will think of myself as a person who is decisive and determined. I expect a good life, and I deserve it. I will be strong and flexible, and see each day as an amazing opportunity. With my children, mate, friends, and coworkers, I'll be a major force for good. I'll triumph over all my fears to reach a place of greater happiness and effectiveness. I'm learning new ways to behave, replacing old ways that are not getting me anywhere."

Learn how to handle your panic attacks smartly

Because you're not yet a graduate of our 30-day anxiety-busting plan, you need to know how to smart-handle a panic attack if you have one. Here are steps to memorize:

1. Know what you're going to say: The minute you begin to experience symptoms, tell yourself that *nothing really bad*

can come from the way your body is reacting. Repeat calming words, such as: "It's okay…it's okay…I'm going to be okay."

2. Breathe deeply: Take deep breaths, very slowly. And think "I'm breathing deeply, slowly, deeply, slowly…"

3. Accept what's happening: Don't try to manhandle it. If you're with a friend or mate, tell that person what you're feeling, and look around you to focus on things in your environment as sources of distraction. Think of the way you would try to distract a small child who's getting into mischief; treat the panic the same way. Expect and welcome the calming effect: "The panic will fade. Now it's fading. It will always fade, and I will not die or go crazy."

4. Calm your odd breathing: If your panic escalates to the point that you hyperventilate (including dizziness, shaking, sweating, or stifled breathing), breathe from your diaphragm slowly and deeply. If there's someone around, ask for a paper bag to breathe into. If not, cup your hands over your nose and mouth to "rebreathe" air. Exhale hard through your mouth; slowly rebreathe through your nose. (See more on diaphragmatic breathing in this chapter.)

Use medication if your doctor recommends a double-whammy approach

Today, many physicians believe that a combination of medication and behavior therapy gives the most relief to those with panic disorder. Patients see results quickly, and they are less likely to relapse. It's entirely possible that your doctor may want you to take a prescription medication, which can be very effective at deterring panic attacks, reducing the frequency you have them or their severity, or preventing them altogether. (See Chapter 1 for more on medications.)

Figure out why you're so anxious

You behave the way you do in reaction to your own unique perceptions of the world around you. Examine your "automatic" knee-jerk thoughts and critique them. List what you do during every waking hour of one day, and put it in columns: Hour one: What I did. Why I did it. How much I liked it, rating it one through 10. Hour two: same things. Then, study your answers. Look for indications that your thinking is distorted. Ask yourself the following:

- Do you find yourself doing things you hate because you feel obligated to please other people?
- Do you have a tendency to demonize people?
- Do you notice a tendency to worsen situations?
- Do you take too much responsibility for making everything right and tidy?
- Do you think you're at the center of everyone's universe and people are always looking at you?
- Do you see things as only good/bad, black/white, instead of expecting some things to be average, neutral, or gray?

If you answered yes to any of the above, you probably have "errors in thinking." You need to work on getting your perception more in tune with reality. In truth, you're *not* always the reason that things go wrong. And, some things people do aren't good or bad—they're either neutral or in-between. Also, remember that most of the time, people are too busy concentrating on themselves to be studying you.

You must figure out how to identify instances of distorted thinking. These are often the villains in panic attacks—the things that give rise to your fears. Extreme worry triggers fast-heart-thumping, which spirals into anxiousness, and then heightened anxiety, and those awful thoughts of dying or going crazy.

Rate your stressors

Begin writing down (journaling) stressful events. Rate each of them. If it's a low stressor, it gets a score of one through five; if it's a high stressor, it gets a score of six through 10. Also, record your specific feelings in regard to the high stressors in your journal.

Tweak your lifestyle

Add about 15 minutes of stretching and moving your body to peaceful and/or upbeat music to your daily routine. And, gradually, make alterations in your diet. Decrease salt and sugar intake.

Decrease alcohol intake. Cut down on caffeine: coffee, colas, and tea. Work into this dietary plan over time—improved nutrition can enhance your overall health and sense of well-being. You don't need to add salt to anything (restaurants and manufacturers add enough salt to foods to meet your daily requirement). You don't need sugar, which pads your body and contributes to irritability. You don't need much caffeine—it nudges your adrenal glands, which pumps up your stress level and makes you agitated. Sometimes, excessive caffeine even contributes to headaches and heart palpitations.

Come up with a yardstick for measuring your progress

Know how you want to feel during a specific time period. You may say, "I will know I'm doing better when I no longer feel very anxious about every social occasion and when I no longer have weekly panic attacks." Or it can be as simple as, "I will be much improved if I'm able to go to the next party I get an invitation to."

Refer to your journal of stressors, and begin working on the ones with high stress ratings. Decide on a goal. After 30 days, where do you want to be in your plan to reduce these stress ratings?

Seek self-understanding

Complete the following sentences, and then carefully scrutinize your answers. (Keep in mind that this is private information that you don't need to share with anyone.)

What I really want for my life is_____.

I think I could be happy if _____.

I wish people understood that I am _____.

I often get anxious when _____.

Most of my panicky feelings revolve around fear that I am going to_____.

Most people think I'm _____.

The best part of me is that I am _____.

What I'd like to work on about me and change, is my tendency to_____.

What I wish I could leave behind me is _____.
A life free of fear would feel _____.

Read over your answers; give them some long, hard thought. Then, savor one important fact: You can have what you want for your life if you release yourself from fear and stop worrying about what other people think of you and what you do. To show that you are willing to invest emotionally in this idea, repeat to yourself: *"I want to be happier. I know that I can't control my life, but I can do things that will improve my chances of a satisfying existence. I promise to accept whatever happens—but I'll do my part."*

• • •

To further get in touch with yourself, try the following exercise:

- Tell someone the thing that you wish people truly understood about you.
- Look at the fear that gives rise to your panic. Decide if it's really going to be a life-or-death situation if you are "revealed" in that way. Do people really care if you do this particular thing? If you do humiliate yourself, as you fear, is that going to be the end of life as you know it?
- Examine what people think about you, and see if it really matters very much that they think this.
- In the previous exercise, you wrote down what you view as the best part of yourself (your kindness, friendliness, sweetness, honesty, humor, and so forth). Check to see if you're sharing this part of you every day.
- You've identified what you would like to change. Now, figure out how to change it. For example, if you'd like to be more organized, look for articles on ways to accomplish this, and do the things suggested. If your flaw is that you're too critical of others, make a point of giving someone the benefit of the doubt, just because he or she is a fellow human being. Whatever needs work, get cracking!
- You know what you'd like to quit thinking about, so tuck it away **right now**. Draw a mental picture of you actually burying "the past."

- Reread your description of what "a life free of fear" would be like. Then, draw a mental picture that you can conjure up when times get tense. For example, you may see yourself lounging like a cat, lying under a big pink umbrella on a beach in Grand Cayman. You're sipping a strawberry drink and you're watching the waves, the colorful people, the yellow sun, and the blue sky. Smell the sunscreen you're smoothing on your limbs. Taste the refreshing, icy drink. Smile at the children playing nearby, as they run and laugh and squiggle their toes in the sand. Call this your "Sun Scene," and be ready to go there at a moment's notice.
- Do what you think it will take to make yourself happier.

• • •

Work on these skills (see instructions in Chapter 3):

- Assertiveness training.
- Defusing demons by sorting beliefs.
- Positive self-talk.

Week Two

During Week Two, you learn "fringe" techniques, visualization, affirmations, and more anxiety-busting skills.

Continue to do your hardy-personality morning self-talk exercise

Add this new twist to your script:

"I'm no one's victim. I'm in charge of what happens every day, and I want to make my days satisfying and meaningful and fun. I'll smile often and laugh a lot."

Use a "fringe" technique when you feel stress welling up inside you

Choose from the following:

1. Take a luxurious bath: Use candles, bath oil or bubble bath, and scented soaps. Settle into the warm water and spoil

yourself with a long, leisurely dip, soothing your mood and muscles. Massage your body, kneading your neck to relax tightness.

2. Listen to music as a form of massage: Choose music that unwinds you: soothing new-age music, such as Enya; soft rock; or classical. Settle into a favorite chair or lie on your bed, and let the music slow your heart rate and decrease your level of anxiety. Use this technique in your car if you have problems with road rage (growing rabid in traffic gridlock). Put on a CD that calms you, and remove yourself mentally from the fray.

Repeat affirmations to feel more in control of stressful situations

Choose one of the following...and repeat it until you completely believe it:

- I am helping myself wind down, feeling more relaxed and calmer than I was only minutes ago.
- I am learning to handle my anxiety and put it behind me.
- I know how to cope with growing anxiety and panic.
- I breathe deeply and slowly, making myself peaceful.
- I am in the moment and enjoying that feeling.
- No situation will bowl me over because I understand how to relax myself.
- I am learning how to unravel negative thoughts and replace them with positive ones that benefit me.
- I have a good life, and it's only getting better.

During this week, frequently practice empowering affirmations:

"I seek to feel totally grounded and alive in the moment. I replace negative thoughts with positive and uplifting ones. I can find a way to handle any situation. I can cope with stressful events effectively."

Use visualization/imagery

Visualize yourself as the most assertive, can-do person on earth. Nothing fazes you; no one's negativity gets to you. If someone faces you with animosity, that person will experience meltdown simply by looking into your peaceful face.

Follow these steps:

1. Find a quiet spot: Begin to breathe deeply. Go slowly.
2. See yourself moving into the situation that has caused you considerable discomfort and panic. For example, you're walking in the door of someone's house to attend a company Christmas party that's "required." Normally, your heart would start pounding and your mouth would dry up. You would think, "Everyone's looking at me and thinking I'm dressed wrong. They can tell that I have nothing to talk about, and everyone will want to avoid me." Anxiety builds, and you're afraid to step into *any* circle of people.
3. Now, play pretend: You did it as a kid and you can do it now. Pretend that you're the most confident person imaginable, and that individual's persona is taking over your body. (In other words, you had a hardy-personality-transplant!) Suddenly, you're *sure* that people want to talk to you. You flash a big smile that dazzles everyone. You step forward and move into a circle and introduce yourself to the first person who looks your way. As your breathing pace escalates, you relax your shoulders. Inhale and exhale slowly. Smile and nod your head to show that you're listening to what your coworker is saying. Adopt a knowing smile that curves up the corners of your lips.
4. Glance into a mind-mirror: Note that you look just like you did leaving the house. Your hair is as good as it gets. Your clothes are clean and pressed and acceptable. Then, make the mirror evaporate, and let that be the last thought you'll have of yourself that evening. Go out and focus on other people—what they're saying, things they're telling you. Really, truly listen and you'll see why certain people become enormous social successes. The fact that they look good is only a small part of what makes them click. What is more important is a person's ability to make someone else feel important and valued—this is the most vital social skill.

Learn diaphragmatic breathing

Diaphragmatic breathing can help you overcome anxiety and correct shallow chest breathing. Usually, when you're anxious, you take shallow, fast breaths, which eventually can lead to hyperventilation. Hyperventilating makes you feel lightheaded and scared; you may tremble and experience tingling in your extremities and lips. You're exhaling too much carbon dioxide compared to the amount of oxygen in your body.

As we said earlier, when you're in a crunch situation and are hyperventilating, the old standard cure is breathing into a paper bag. It works because you're breathing back in the carbon dioxide you exhale into the bag, and thus restoring balance. But it's good to know how to breathe diaphragmatically—a good calming technique for all times. Here are the steps:

1. Close your eyes. Breathe in slowly through your nose, and count to four in your mind. Imagine that you see fresh air going down into your stomach. Place your hand on your stomach, and feel the expansion.
2. Slowly breathe out (exhale) through your mouth; count to four in your mind. Picture air leaving your stomach until all is gone. Say the word "relax."
3. Open your eyes.
4. Go through these steps several times to get the hang of it.

When you start to hyperventilate, go back through these steps. When you feel like a panic attack is coming on, start this technique as soon as possible.

Each day, practice a bit. You're freed of some anxiety because you now have a way to conquer hyperventilating the next time you feel threatened by a panic attack.

Learn these skills (see instructions in Chapter 3):

- Changing responses to cues (reframing).
- Improving social skills.
- Fine-tuning relationship-building.
- Anger management.

Week Three

Expand your sense of self in Week Three by doing the following:

Enhance your hardy-personality self-talk

For your morning hardy-personality talk, add these lines:

"I won't let people run over me. I can express my needs and expect those who love me to respond. In turn, I want to meet the needs of my family and friends and coworkers, but I will look at the 'cost' of fulfilling their requests. I will not be a martyr who does things people want me to, despite the heavy toll it takes on me or my health."

Identify the trigger factors and reinforcing factors that have gotten you to an anxiety-ridden place

Certain elements of your lifestyle are probably players in your anxiety problem. To find out if that is the case, answer the following:

1. Do you feel boxed-in by anxiousness because your mate is a huge factor in your stress?
2. Do you justify behavior that's totally unacceptable from a parent or mate or child?
3. Do your panic attacks make your mate (or parent or child) give you attention that you ordinarily don't get?
4. Do others contribute to your image of yourself as "helpless" and pathetic?

You need to "fix" trigger factors and reinforcing factors that have helped to make you an anxious person. To do that, you'll have to decondition yourself (or "unlearn") current negative behaviors.

An example: Let's say your mate's constant criticism is turning you into a sullen figure who is always walking on eggshells. The criticism is a trigger factor.

Or perhaps you let a grown son mistreat you, steal your money (and your pride) and you make excuses for him (if his dad hadn't been indifferent, the kid wouldn't be so messed up).

Or you're the "forgotten" and boring member of the family, who now gets attention because people want to hear about your "interesting" panic attacks. They baby you, helping you settle into a panic pattern by reinforcing the situation.

It's time to use "reality therapy." If much of your anxiety stems from a mate or parent who is a major negative influence, confront that truth and figure out how to express what you need from him or her. If that person is unresponsive, distance yourself for a period of time while you work on getting healthier.

Desensitize yourself from feeling anxious
by approaching your feared situation in tiny, careful pieces

Use a firm, anxiety-busting mind-set to guide you. To desensitize yourself, take on small exposures to the stimulus that usually makes you very anxious. Call on your "calming karma" to counter the negativity.

Make a list of steps for working up to the major fear gradually. Let's look at treating a fear of flying. These are the steps you would take in order to desensitize yourself to the fear:

1. Look at airline advertisements in a magazine (at home).
2. Watch a movie that has passengers in a plane.
3. Go to the airport and watch planes take off.
4. Think over the answer you'll give to your fearful thoughts the next time you feel that way.
5. Make yourself an index card with these words on it: "Yes, you can fly. No, you won't die. In a few hours, you'll be on the ground again, and the anxious feelings will be behind you."
6. Go to the airport and watch people coming and going, and think of the way they're anticipating trips and telling friends of their adventures.
7. Plan a trip. As you call for flight reservations, regulate your nervous breathing.
8. On the day of your departure, repeat your affirmations and visualize yourself getting off the plane with a smile on your face—satisfied that you conquered your fear and happy to be going somewhere.

9. Preflight, when you're sitting in the plane, talk to the person next to you about the weather or shuffle cards. Use diaphragmatic breathing as needed.

10. During takeoff, get out your index-card sign and read it. Squeeze the exercise ball you've brought along. Deep breathe. Retreat mentally to your "Sun Scene" until the plane reaches a high altitude and settles into place.

11. When it's time for the plane to land, go back through squeezing your exercise ball, glancing at your sign.

12. At your airport destination, reward yourself: buy a chocolate malt, T-shirt, rent a high-end rental car, or enjoy a special dinner.

Do these steps until you feel the "fear" has been defused, and you've become empowered.

● ● ●

Through this exercise, you will expose yourself to the physical symptoms—the dizziness, the lightheaded feeling—by inducing these purposely. Then, you're able to work on changing your responses to them. Instead of assuming that dizziness equals losing your mind, you label it accurately "I feel dizzy—no more, no less. I'll get past it."

You *can* learn to respond in new ways to situations that scare you. New responses replace your old distorted responses. Take this part in small doses.

For a fear of rising water, for example, you can make yourself run an errand the next time it rains and the streets have an inch of water. This trip should be a short distance so that you can bite off just enough to give you a taste of the fear, but not an overwhelming amount. When you experience bizarre thoughts and you expect to be hit with the usual physical symptoms, stop the thought by using planned self-talk. "Yes, there's water in the street, but no, it's not a flood. I won't drown, die, or lose control of my car. I'm going to be fine."

Gradually, increase the challenge until you finally feel ready to handle the real test—streets that have standing water of rather scary proportions. Of course, don't be silly and venture into water that no sensible person would enter. But during a normal downpour—what would have frightened you senseless in the past—get in your car and practice fording the streams in the streets. Expect to feel your fingers clinching the steering wheel—that's quite okay. Just accept that you feel uptight.

The difference here is that you're no longer allowing avoidance to run your life. You're out on the road, working to beat your fear of rising water. Your new motto could be: "Even though I still feel anxiety, I know I'm not in physical danger, and that I'll be all right. So what if I feel a little anxious? I won't die—I'll get home in one piece."

What happens now? You begin to get a handle on a situation that used to have you totally confused. Knowing what to do, you reduce your anxiety in advance, and that makes the truth hit home at last—you realize that you really don't need to arrange your life to avoid what you fear doing. You still can, of course—but it's not necessary, and besides, it's a bother!

Three times a week, take a nature walk alone or with a partner—spouse, child, or friend

Wear comfy tennis shoes and walk a mile or two through a park or your neighborhood. You'll get some exercise, but you're also out to recapture a sense of childlike wonder at your environment.

Kick back and let nature's wonders amaze you just like a baby joyfully discovers a perfect blade of grass. Look at branches of trees. Note the colors of changing seasons in leaves and flowers. Smell the magnolias, roses, and honeysuckle vines. Experience the balmy atmosphere of a spring day. Observe the hues of people's clothing. Delight in people's idiosyncrasies. Listen for the sounds of your streets: the cars' horns, the children's squeals, the dogs' barks—everything.

Imagine a breeze wafting away all of your anxiety, and replacing it with calm and peace.

Pinpoint "togetherness role models"

Emulate people who are successful examples of what you would like to achieve. If you want to be good at marriage, study couples who have happy marriages. If you want to be a good parent, watch people who are good parents. If you admire a person's work ethic and success, see how that person pulls it off. Don't be afraid to ask for advice or tips from those you admire.

Strive for an overall state of preparedness

You'll feel less anxious if you prepare yourself for situations that ordinarily make you anxious. For tips, refer to the 100 common anxiety situations, on page 117 and then examine the ways you can prepare yourself to handle these.

Work on these skills (see instructions in Chapter 3):

- Anger management.
- Learning to avoid blame-shifting.
- Effective need-expression.

Week Four

You're heading into the home stretch, so pull out all the stops and use as many of your newly learned skills as necessary to defuse anxiety.

Tweak your self-talk script (for your mornings) to reflect how you're feeling about your newly empowered self

Change your daily self-talk to establish firmly your new attitude. Try something like the following:

"I don't worry as much as I used to. I'm not letting fears dictate my decisions. I'm a stronger person who no longer lets anxiety ruin many of my waking hours. I look at problems as challenges and I feel as if I'm becoming a good problem-solver. I know how to 'get outside of myself' and focus on other people."

Use your mastery of thought-stopping and cognitive restructuring

Every time a negative thought starts hanging out in your head, put a stop to it. Use thought-stopping to banish the thought, and replace it with a positive, can-do idea.

When you do feel a panic attack creeping up—or you actually suffer one—look at what happened. Use cognitive restructuring to figure out the chain of events that led up to the panic...and how you'll solve your problem the next time. Take apart the thoughts that led you to trouble, and dismantle them. Did you go crazy? Did people laugh at you? Did you die?

Reduce the focus on yourself by reaching out

Volunteer to help a neighbor, a center for the homeless, a shelter for children, or other charitable activity. Use what you have—time, energy, storytelling—to give something to someone who needs help. Call a community center, church, or city hall, and inquire about volunteer opportunities. Then, get yourself moving—strike out this very day and sign up to be a volunteer who gives a few hours of every week to doing something for others, for no pay other than the reward of having helped.

List things you'd still like to do to upgrade your life

Be realistic about your options. If you're living in a situation that isn't getting better, be honest with yourself. Quit saying "Oh, my husband hits me because I make him mad—it's my fault. He's really a very good man." The truth is, you don't have to live a hellish existence—you *can* find a way to leave and improve your life. Give yourself permission to seek happiness; no one has to be a doormat for an abusive spouse, child, or supervisor.

Add an imagery and relaxation technique to your stress-relieving repertoire

To be anxious in the first place, you have to be imaginative. And, that will come in handy when you want to induce a state of relaxation. (Anxious people are especially good at coaching themselves in relaxation techniques.)

Follow the steps listed below:

- Think of a movie you found so engrossing that you were hardly aware of events or people around you. Or, recall a time that you were so lost in thought while driving that you arrived at a destination and wondered how you got there. This "altered state of consciousness" is like hypnosis.

- Now, close your eyes and relax. Breathe deeply and think of yourself floating.
- Key in on your "Sun Scene"—the pleasant getaway place that's remarkable for its serenity, peacefulness, and comfort. Yours may be a beach. Some people float on clouds. Others retreat to a treehouse.
- Continue making your dream scenario as engrossing as possible, and lose yourself in it totally.

Learn these skills (see specifics in Chapter 3):

- Thought-stopping.
- Role-playing/visualization.
- Inoculating against stressors.

Are we there yet? Am I "hardy" enough?

You've done the work and completed the plan.

At the end of the 30 days, step back and assess your progress. Hopefully, you have reduced your anxiety by honing hardy personality traits.

To assess how far you have come, refer to your yardstick of progress. "I will be much improved if I'm able to go to the next party I get an invitation to." So, did you go? Were you able to enjoy it, get outside of yourself, and get to know other people?

Check for signs that you've accomplished what you set out to do. If you need to brush up on some of your skills, do that. Get a feel for how far you've come—and give yourself credit for trying and for making progress.

Test your new-and-improved 'hardy' personality

Answer the following true-false questions, and compare your current feelings about these things to the way you thought about the same issues 30 days ago:

1. Overall, I like who I am.
2. I'm not very worried about what people think about me.
3. I do what I need to do and am less likely to look over my shoulder to see what people are thinking of my actions.
4. I realize that others have reasons for acting the way they do and these may have absolutely nothing to do with me.
5. I know exactly what I'll do the next time I feel panic growing in me.
6. I'm not letting fear lead me around anymore, and that feels good.
7. I'm enjoying volunteer work. Helping others who are less fortunate helps me keep things in proper perspective.
8. When mistakes from my past begin to haunt me, I get up and do something productive. I don't dwell on history.
9. I am more open than I used to be. My closed-off days are behind me.
10. I'm not as hard on myself as I used to be.
11. I feel like a stronger person than I used to, and I like the way that feels.
12. I don't let people push me around, but if someone doesn't like me, I steer clear of that person. Not everyone has to like me and I don't have to like everyone.
13. I say what I want, in a nice way.
14. I no longer expect people to read my mind.
15. I understand that people are too wrapped up in themselves to be scrutinizing me as hard as I once thought they were.
16. I'm less judgmental and critical than I used to be.
17. I don't feel like my blushing and stammering are huge mistakes.
18. People who will do anything to win don't bother me much.
19. If I do something to embarrass myself, I know that I'll get over it; I won't die from embarrassment.
20. My personality is hardier than it used to be—I'm not filled with fear.

If you answered "true" to 13-20 of these, you're in great shape! Kudos to you! You've truly "hardied up" your personality. This puts you in a great position for leaving panic attacks behind.

If you answered "true" to eight to 12, you're making progress, but you still have a little bit more work to do to be a panic-free personality.

Seven or fewer "trues" and you need to go back to the tips in Week One and review if you've gone through every step and truly digested what you're supposed to do.

Kara tries the 30-day plan

Week One

With a copy of *No More Panic Attacks* in hand, Kara* decided to start each day with 15 minutes of stretching to music. After that, she journaled her stressors. This is what she wrote: an alcoholic husband, the recent death of her father, and event-planning (a baby shower).

She also set up her yardstick for measuring progress: "I'll know I'm better when I know how to handle my fears without having panic attacks and worrying that I'm going to die."

Kara confronted two distorted thinking patterns that she recognized as hers: a tendency to turn situations into catastrophes and an overly exaggerated feeling of responsibility for keeping everything "right" and tidy. She began to study assertiveness training, defusing demons by sorting beliefs, and positive self-talk.

Week Two

When Kara felt a panic attack coming on, she stopped it by using the breathing techniques she had learned. She tried visualization and affirmations.

She sorted her shower-planning thoughts into "logical" and "illogical" piles. She had been afraid that nothing she could cook would be "good enough" for the people she was inviting, some of whom were high-profile. She could hire a caterer, but that would mean blowing her budget. Besides, how would she know which one was *the right* caterer? She agonized over the possibility that no one would come—a fear that came from the memory of a friend who gave her 5-year-old a birthday party and no one came. That was many years ago, but Kara still felt bad for that child.

To calm herself, she used a luxury bath to decompress. She listened to jazz as she lay in the Jacuzzi.

Kara studied her stressors and her reactions to them. She began seeing the fallacies in her shower-planning fears. First, she admitted that she could cook, but because she had a very busy professional life and two children, they mostly ate out, so she lacked confidence in her cooking. She decided to hire a caterer and do an extra freelance job to cover the expenses. To find a good caterer, she called a friend who did PR for restaurants. She made one phone call and had a list of three caterers. Kara attacked her guest-list fear by looking at the people she was inviting and estimating the likelihood of their attending. She communicated with those who were invited and sent out invitations early enough (but not too early). The shower went well—plenty of guests, a happy honoree, and a slightly uptight hostess.

Kara also worked on dealing with the death of her father. Her sadness had become such a distraction that she couldn't concentrate; she had insomnia and heart palpitations. She decided to expose herself to reality gradually. She began by getting out a few pictures of her father and a ring he had given her. A few days later, responding to her mother's request to help clean out his closet, she sorted clothing for Goodwill, and set aside mementos. They cried and talked about special moments.

She found that her spouse tired quickly of hearing her talk about her sadness, so she e-mailed a girlfriend when she needed a comforting word. Kara began taking nature walks. She "redefined" herself in the new context of a life in which her father was no longer alive. Her dad had raised her to be a confident, happy young woman. She told herself, "I'm going to be all right because my father raised me to love life. To honor him, I will make my days count."

A new problem intruded: Her husband screamed at her and raged at the kids. One night he pounded her with verbal abuse until she asked him to leave. He was so drunk he fell down. The children were crying. His head was bleeding because he had stumbled and hit the edge of the coffee table. Kara made sure he was all right, called his sister to come be with him, and she packed their bags and left with the children.

She kept telling herself she was a capable woman who could handle this situation. Thinking "hardy" and "in-charge" carried Kara through the trauma until she was set up in a hotel and could put her kids to bed and then collapse and go to sleep.

Week Three

Kara had more stress than she had experienced in the past year, but she felt more on top of things. Helplessness was replaced with belief that she could overcome problems. She was working on seeing challenges as opportunities.

Kara journaled her experiences, and drew a family picture of things before (how they had been) and after (how she wanted them to be when their situation improved). She realized that her husband was a "trigger factor" who had lent anxiety to her life; she had made excuses for him, rationalizing his unacceptable behavior so that she wouldn't have to make decisions.

She tried to get her husband to go to counseling, but he refused, agreeing only that they should separate. She got custody of the children and met with a lawyer to make things official. Her children began going on walks with her.

For her role model of togetherness, Kara chose Laura Bush. She admired the way the First Lady had risen to the occasion of being a calming force during the months following the September 11 disasters.

To follow the guideline of "preparedness," Kara joined a single-parents' support group, and searched on the Internet for sources of inexpensive legal advice.

Week Four

Kara still experienced panic symptoms, but reduced them by using diaphragmatic breathing and self-talk. She had a bad habit of negative self-talk, but thought-stopping helped her.

She needed more self-confidence. Living with an alcoholic had given her feelings of isolation and low self-esteem. Kara hated that she'd let friendships lapse because she had concentrated on her career when it seemed like the only thing that made sense in her life.

She wanted to get back to seeing friends. And she hoped to expand her profession. As a graphic artist, she wanted to freelance so she could be at home when her kids got out of school. To make this work, she would have to learn more computer skills. She knew a friend who had a computer-whiz buddy and she hired him to teach her.

In Week Four, Kara reinforced new ways of avoiding panic attacks. She had been successful, so far. But still looming in the back of her mind were those horribly debilitating fears:

- What if my husband starts coming around to bother my family?
- What if I don't get enough work to support my family?
- What if my kids suffer from not seeing their dad enough?
- What if I'm just not as good without my father around?

Each thought would make her anxious. She would expect a racing heart, fatigue, jumpiness, dry mouth, and tight throat.

Here's where the true test of the 30-day anxiety-busting plan came into play. Kara was avoiding seeing friends but she tried replacing her faulty thought patterns with constructive ones. When she told herself, "I'll make everyone depressed if I go around my friends," she forced herself to challenge the statement, "No, it's *not* true that I will make everyone feel depressed—*not every single person*. Maybe just a few. In fact, my friends may enjoy seeing me."

Kara set a lunch date with a friend, rescheduled it twice, then went. She thus exposed herself to gradually increasing anxiety, and saw that it was not as bad as imagined.

Finally, she faced her most feared situation—a meeting with her husband and his attorney. Before leaving home, Kara visualized herself going through the meeting, being positive, and surviving it. When her fists clinched, she relaxed them. She took a deep breath, and thought of the meeting as an adventure in learning how to handle any kind of anxious situation.

In the meeting, each time a toxic thought came to mind, she pressed her forefinger on the corner of her eye, as a signal to banish the unwanted thought. It worked. She shifted to positive communication.

She repeated her goals mentally:

Be open but tactful. Listen to what is important to the other person, and consider his views carefully. Look for points that can be negotiated. Find ways to give strokes by using language such as, "You made a good point" and "I would like to find a way to work this out."

She also started doing volunteer work at a community center where she read to vision-impaired seniors. The work took her to a joyful place, so that she looked forward to Thursday nights. She was called the "young one" at the center, which 40-year-old Kara found amusing.

In assessing her month, Kara summed it up this way: "I'm far more comfortable with my life than I was a month ago. I can't handle absolutely everything, but I have skills to use when I get scared. I like to think a situation out to its 'worst possible' outcome, and make sure that's something I'm braced to handle. I know that I'm a lucky woman with lots of advantages, and I don't want to panic my life away. I'd have to say the 30 days of anxiety-busting absolutely helped me."

Now, it's your turn

Go to Week One and get started! And anytime you feel shaky, play Leeann Womack's song "I Hope You Dance." It's a great theme for ridding yourself of fear, and absolutely loving every breath that you take.

5

What to Do When Your Children Make You Anxious

Anxiety-Busting Tools for This Chapter
- Thought-stopping.
- Defusing demons by sorting beliefs.
- Positive self-talk.

NOTE: THE SUBJECT OF PARENTING IS VERY COMPLEX; THUS, THE TIPS offered here mainly hit the high points. For in-depth information, see a book on parenting.

Your child curses and smart-mouths you

Ann* was experiencing panic attacks. The trigger was the mean mouth of her 15-year-old daughter, who had become an unrecognizable creature when she'd turned 14. The kid who had once been sweet and fun had turned into a monster of scary contradictions. One day she was angry; the next day, she was secretive; finally, she would rage and shout obscenities. Ann was shocked when her daughter smart-mouthed her. She tried, unsuccessfully, to make her stop. This made Ann feel anxious, as if she'd lost control.

To cope with this problem, parents need to get up to speed on one disturbing fact—nasty is in. Mean-as-cool-behavior has been glamorized on television via MTV and the WWE, leaving the impression (correct, by the way) that broadcasting is using pop-culture icons to "condition" young people and mold them in a way that will make them avid consumers of TV-touted values and merchandise. Down-and-dirty 'attitude' has become cool, and parents are left to face the spin-offs of a cultural wave of trendy-hatefulness.

So, first, try to understand that smart-mouthing and cursing translate very differently to your child. To you, it feels like sabotage and cruel-and-unusual treatment. However, your teen really may just be dabbling in the behaviors she sees on television, in movies, and at school. People aren't nice to each other, and in the same way that the slang that goes along with it finds its way into the dictionary, mean-spiritedness has snaked its way into the behavior of youth. Furthermore, the growing-up years of 12 to 18 are difficult ones, when your child is moving from being a dependent child to finding her way as a fledgling adult. The rough adjustment makes adolescence a tough time.

But even though smart-mouth kids aren't unusual these days, you can't tolerate this kind of behavior. Actions have consequences. Don't let bad behavior slide.

So, try these ideas for curbing your anxiety while smoothing out the wrinkles in your smart-mouthed child:

- Know what to expect.
- Fine-tune your coping skills (see Chapter 3).
- Learn "lines" that will serve your needs.

This is a time during child-rearing when the phrase "less is more" has the most meaning. Try to be with your teen (often). Serve as a sounding board. Be supportive. But choose your words carefully and listen more than you talk.

Here are 10 ways to negotiate the teen years:

1. Have your own life

Just like you always suspected, you're entitled to a good life even though you have a teen in the house. And no matter what kind of dysfunction your child has, make sure it doesn't ruin your life. Your teen may be your darling, all right, but hopefully you have other things that matter, too: a mate, family, friends, work, church, activities, among others. Don't let your sun rise or fall by the craziness of your teen's antics.

2. Accept reality

The little kid who once loved being with you is now moving into a wider sphere of influence. You, as the parent, still matter immensely to your teen, but that's a best-kept secret, not for public consumption. Make no mistake: You're loved intensely by your teen—but showing that vulnerability is terribly uncool right now.

Furthermore, your teen is judging you. Gone are the days when your clothes, sayings, and home-decorating were simply wonderful because you were Mom or Dad. Now, a teen looks warily at everything you do. Maybe, just maybe, you're not quite as neat and keen as she once thought. You are, even worse, a possible source of embarrassment in your teen's pool of friends. Don't get bent over this very natural and normal transitioning to adulthood.

And guess what? If you fall short on her coolness-scale, no problem! You're not a teen and you're not trying to be (if you are, that's a whole different book). Hopefully, you have your style, and teens have their own, and all parties should respect the others' choices.

3. Accept that secretive behavior is perfectly normal for teens

Establishing a degree of autonomy means stepping back as a parent. Taking you into every confidence would be quite unusual at this age. However, even though your child acts like a CIA operative (huge secrets to hide), don't invade your teen's privacy. No diary-reading, letter-skimming, perusing of notebooks—and don't barge into your teen's bedroom without knocking. These are trust-breakers. You shouldn't snoop in your child's room or private things unless you have good reason to believe that he or she is into drug or alcohol abuse. And this should be used as a last resort after you've exhausted all other means of communication.

4. Say what you feel to your child

Say what you feel when your child does something that's praise-worthy, or something that disappoints you. When your child is rude or abrasive, tell him or her exactly how it makes you feel. Instead of name-calling ("When did you turn into such a brat?") calmly state, with total seriousness, how very hurtful those words are. Tell your teen it makes you sad to have your own child, whom you love dearly, treat you with disdain. This has a sobering effect. It is straightforward. It is heartfelt. It hits at the core of teenspeak (they're the ones who are always demanding to cut the BS).

5. Search for opportunities to praise

Look for opportunities to give your child a pat on the back. Right now, your teen may feel as if most of the world is lined up against him or her—but that won't be too awful if you are your teen's ally, unwaveringly patient and loving.

Never forget that teens are shaky. Their emotions are near the surface much of the time. No matter how mature, cute, smart, or confident your child may seem, underneath that fragile façade is a frightened, unsure mini-adult who is testing his wings every day and getting mixed cues. That's why your validation, at every turn, can serve to build a strong bond that will endure the changing winds of adolescence.

When you see your teen—before or after school—see how she responds when you're generous with praise about her clothes, style, smile, or whatever. Get in your teen's corner. Be a staunch supporter. Let your teen know that no one in her life is more encouraging.

By this point, you may be doubtful about our advice. Why, you ask, should you team up with this gnarly teen-wolf who curses you? Where's the sense in that? One thing's for sure—you're the adult in this equation. You're the one who really should "act mature." You're the grown-up.

You must maintain sanity and serenity. And you're better equipped to upgrade flawed communication (cursing, smart-mouthing, etc.) with *someone who likes you* than with someone who hates the sight of you. Stay upbeat. Stay calm. Unflappable is your marching order.

Remind yourself that teen years are temporary. What's important is coming out on the other side of this difficult period with a strong relationship intact. Tell your child that is exactly what you're working toward, and ask her to help you achieve that goal.

The next time your teen strikes out at you with curses, ask, "What's really bothering you? Do you want to talk?"

She may snap back, *"You're* what's bothering me! And no, I don't want to talk to *you."* Stay calm. Reiterate that if she ever wants to unload feelings or anything else on you, you're ready and willing to listen. Then add, "If you can tell me what I'm doing that bothers you, specifically, I'll work on it, I promise. No one could care more about what you think than I do."

Continue to give your child positive feedback. "I loved the way I heard you talking to your dad on the phone. You sounded so interested in how tired he was, working long hours at the office. I'm happy to know I've raised a child who cares about other people." Another example: "I love that you're a good listener. When I talk to you, I always feel like you're taking in every word I say."

6. Never take the approach that teens hate most: "Me: mighty parent; you: dumb kid"

If you find yourself about to say, "stop backtalking me because I said so" or "you'll do as I say as long as you're under my roof," remember how you loathed those words when you were a kid. Instead, tell your son or daughter you don't want to be talked to in that way because it's disrespectful and hurtful. Tell your child that you would like to be treated as respectfully as you treat him. Hopefully, your treatment of your child is right-on-target. Don't expect your teen to be nice to you if that's not the way you treat him. Contempt breeds contempt.

7. Play up the good stuff

When your child does speak to you in a respectful, kind way, point it out and thank her for it. That advice may sound moronic, but try it—it works. Praise good efforts and you'll get a lot more of them.

8. Make home a place of comfort and security

When your child gets home from school and wants to spout off about things that were bothersome during the day, be encouraging. Allow your frustrated teen to talk. Listen; be supportive and uncritical. It's okay for him to be mad. If there are problems with a teacher and your teen thinks he is being treated unfairly, take his side and present a united front. Show your child that you're willing to go to school for a teacher-parent conference and try to iron out problems. Teachers *can* be wrong, and many do not meet students' needs. Ask any teacher you know and they'll admit the awful truth: Some educators hate kids.

9. Be confident and unwavering about the rules

Explain exactly *why* you set a rule if your teen questions it. Be fair. And if your child fails to live up to a rule, have a talk and ask what kind of punishment your teen would mete out if she had a child who broke the rules. Discuss punishment and come up with something that both of you agree is fair for the offense. Grounding does not have to be in your vocabulary—it has become such a cliché. It rarely works well in doing anything...other than alienating your teen.

10. Talk frankly about your expectations about smoking, alcohol, drugs, and sex

Discuss things such as dating and curfews. Allow your teen to have opinions that are different from yours—no matter how radical they are. You have to let her have thoughts of her own; she isn't you. Be encouraging to show that you're listening. Nod and say "yes" and "really?" Sit where you can make eye contact. Mirror back to your child what you believe you've heard. Don't interrupt. And try to arrive at a platform on these issues that you both can accept and agree on; don't take a dictatorial approach. Let your teen have a say and you'll be much more likely to draw some cooperation.

You can't go on dates with your daughter or control your son's actions, so your best hope is to develop some self-discipline. Remember, that's the only kind of discipline that will go on to college.

Don't forget that a young person's concerns and thoughts are real and valid, and must not be dismissed summarily. Treat your teen at least as well as you would a close friend of yours. If you hear yourself snapping at your kid, you need a reminder—*that's not the way people talk to each other when they like each other* (much less, love each other).

Every single day of your son's or daughter's life, express your love. Say that you feel unbelievably lucky that he or she is your child. It's the most important thing you can do.

• • •

When Ann tried these ideas, she was able to set up a new code for teen behavior in her home. Her daughter helped. Together, they wrote an agreement. And today, they have fewer disagreements, no cursing, and a higher level of respect. Ann no longer has panic attacks, and she feels optimistic about her relationship with her daughter.

You're anxiety-ridden because you're a single parent

Single parenting can be tough. But there are many ways to take the stressful pain away and replace it with joy. Refer to the section on relationship-building (Chapter 3) and try the following ideas for improving the bond you have with your child:

- Show respect for your child. Give him or her the kindness you would a close friend. (Why should your child get any less?)
- Point out what you like about your child, along with the things that you think make your child special. Children whose parents appreciate them, and show their appreciation, flourish.
- Show an interest in things your child likes. For example, just because today's music for teens doesn't thrill you doesn't mean you should thumb your nose at it. Instead, celebrate that your child has found music that brings her joy. Picking it apart will do little to improve your relationship—it will only alienate her. Don't make fun of her taste.
- Give praise for good efforts. Look for opportunities to thank and congratulate your youngster for feeding the dog, doing chores, and so forth.
- Share your thoughts on various issues when you're in the car together or when taking a walk. But, don't be the "big lecturer" delivering a sermon. Your kid will learn to tune you out in a hurry.
- Have fun. Laugh. Sing. Dance. Be silly.
- Avoid giving the impression that you only like her when she makes good grades or scores a home run. Show unconditional

love. You should love your son when he gets a traffic ticket or when your daughter goes to detention. And be on your kid's side in trying to make sure mistakes aren't repeated. You love your kids when they are grumpy. You love them when they're on the outs with every friend they have. You welcome them with comfort, open-arms, and love, unfaltering in your love and support.

You're worried about your child's drug or alcohol problem

You've watched actor Robert Downey, Jr.'s drug drama played out on the news, as he gets "cured" and then spirals back down into the pit of user's despair.

Obviously, you don't want your child to go through the hellishness of fighting an addiction. But let's start with the premise that a problem already exists. You've seen the signs, and you know your young adult needs help. And this drug and/or alcohol problem is causing you anxiety, as it is for the entire family...not to mention what your teen is going through.

You should start by consulting with mental health/drug rehab experts about intervention and possible inpatient treatment—that will give your teen several weeks removed from drugs and alcohol. In a licensed facility designed for rehabilitation, your child can receive psychological guidance intended to get to the root of what made him or her turn to drugs or alcohol: low self-esteem, peer pressure, fondness for the taste, boredom, whatever.

On the other hand, if you think your child has just begun experimenting with drugs, be proactive. Lead your kid firmly away from drugs and/or alcohol in a way that is supportive and loving (even if it takes some time for your teen to acknowledge that).

With the young person who has dabbled in drugs, try this approach, which really works when done consistently. You must first tell your child you want to "partner" with him or her. Figure out what has changed in your teen's life. When talking with your teen, try these steps in reality therapy:

1. "How are you feeling about what's going on in your life?" you'll ask, broaching the subject in a sincere way (with no sarcasm). "You seem different, and your grades are pretty dismal. I've been wondering how you feel about these changes?" Remember, keep the focus on your child, not on your feelings or the repercussions for you. This is your child's life, and your kid will be affected the most by poor decisions. Your teen's drug/alcohol use also affects you and the rest of the family. However, you can expect to see an easing of your burden when you shift your mental frame of reference to thinking of the "problem" as your child's.

2. Discuss the drug and alcohol use as a given—something you know that is happening—not as a hypothetical. You both know there's a problem. Be matter-of-fact in saying that you want to get it out on the table and look at it. Don't act like it's the end of the world or that your teen is making you miserable and suicidal.

3. Let your child talk. You want to get his thoughts on how life is different from the way it used to be. Listen, staying unflappable, no matter what he says, even if it's something like this: "Now that I'm a big drinker, I have more fun. I have cooler friends. I don't mind making bad grades."

4. Then, when it's your turn to talk, tell your kid you're worried that drugs and alcohol will make life difficult and horrible for him. Ask only to be heard.

Explain that it seems to you that his only emphasis is "today's fun," giving little thought to the future. You're concerned that there is no thinking ahead at all. How does your teen think he will earn a living? Tell him that, typically, people with drug and alcohol problems have trouble keeping jobs because they aren't dependable.

Tell him that you worry because drugs and alcohol make a person's judgment cloudy. Many more car wrecks with teens happen because of drinking and drugging drivers. Hazy minds sometimes lead to risk-taking.

If your teen is female, point out that girls have to be wary about drinking alcohol that might contain a date-rape drug, such as GHB (commonly known as "roofies").

Make your child aware that you're also concerned that drug use may spiral into "heavier" options, which can put many people on a lifelong disaster track, as is the case with many crack or heroin addicts.

Admit that you know these are the dark sides of drugs—things that not every drug-user or alcohol-user ends up doing. All you're asking is that your teen should try to look at the possibilities without rose-colored glasses.

Ask your teen to write a list of the pluses and minuses of drugs and alcohol so that she can consider what's really going on. You want your child to do this for her own benefit, not for you. Remind your teen that this talk is about love, and not about control.

Now, shift your focus. Turn away from dwelling on your child's problem to examine the anxiety you're living with daily as a result of your teen's poor choices. This is something you can definitely do something about.

Naturally, your guilt is super-sized. You're hit, night and day, thinking "where did I go wrong?" These thoughts fill your mind and heart, and threaten to become the only lucid moments you have all day.

Here are some skills that come in handy when a parent is dealing with a young person who's into alcohol or drugs:

- Thought-stopping. Get rid of the nonproductive thinking that beats you up with guilt. That won't help you summon up the poise and calm that you need to deal with the situation like an adult.

- Changing your responses to cues. Think of the realities: the things you can do to help the addict and your family. Get your child help from a mental health professional or licensed rehab program. Don't focus on your child's reluctance to hear what you are saying. Do everything you can to put a positive tilt on conversations, "I'm sure you just need time to consider the pros and cons and make a good choice."

Emphasize your love and faith in your teen, not your disappointment. If you attack with negatives, she will turn away for good, leaving you unable to help at all. Work hard to keep the lines of communication open. That way, you can help steer your child to professional help in shaking the addiction.

You're feeling anxious because your grown kid is very inconsiderate

You ask: "When did my little darling sprout horns and a devil's tail?" Visions of the precious little 4-year-old come to mind, and you grow so nostalgic that it clouds your perspective. But you're also angry—something's definitely wrong. Your grownup kid, for whom you have made so many sacrifices, is now virtually spitting in your face.

But, this happens, and you have every right to feel mad.

Many people have experiences with their grown children that they don't deserve. But right now, you need to figure out how to cope. Hopefully, your child's attitude may change as a result of your reinvented attitude.

Use thought-stopping. Stop obsessing about the awful outcomes of this behavior. Eliminate thoughts like "he's going to end up in the gutter," "she'll go to jail for sure," or "he'll go to hell." Instead, react to what's really happening.

For example, let's say you co-signed a car note for your 25-year-old son, and now the car has been repossessed and your credit is ruined. Every time you think of it, you feel extremely resentful, which only ramps up your unhappiness.

So, tell yourself this: "The repo happened, and I got mad about it, but I refuse to live in the past and keep reexperiencing it. I'll admit that I'm disappointed that my child would do this, that I doubt his sense of responsibility, but I won't let it ruin my life. It isn't worth living with a feeling of doom and sadness because of bad credit. And it's also not worth a grudge against your child."

However, you should address with your child how this whole incident affected you...and that your credit is ruined. Emphasize that there are consequences to his decisions and that they can affect him and other people.

Focus on what you can do: Refuse to be a co-signer for him again. Ask him to pay back what he owes you. Tell him you love him even though he makes mistakes. Let him know you never stop loving him.

You're experiencing anxiety because your son or daughter is leaving home

Your grown child is excited about crossing over the grand threshold of college-life or marriage, and you're acting pitifully, thumbing through old photo albums and scrapbooks. You never thought it would be over—the parenting thing. But the truth is that it's not. Of course you're going to see a change in parent-child dynamics because you'll be dealing in a more mature manner, but this is your child, and that doesn't change with his new autonomy. He will still be turning to you for comfort, advice, help, friendship, and if your kid is off to college (not marriage), you'll still be getting phone calls for money.

Take the focus off the gloominess of your "empty nest" by trying one (or all) of these three things:

1. You've always been too busy to do volunteer work, but now you have time. If you get involved with a program such as Big Brothers/Big Sisters, a local women's shelter, or some other worthy cause, your life will be so full of rewarding moments that it will shrink your child's absence.

2. Develop new hobbies. Most of us have things on that list of things we'd do if we had the time...and now's when you get to review those possibilities. Have you always talked about taking piano lessons? Do you want to hire a personal trainer to help you get in better shape? Was there a book you wanted to write?

3. Meet some new friends. When your life was filled with playdates, sleepovers, and chauffeuring, you weren't worried about meeting new people. In fact, most busy parents do well to keep old friendships intact. But now you have time to nurture friendships, do lunch, and join a club. By concentrating on others—the best way to make and keep new friends—you'll relieve the stress of empty-nest syndrome. Focus on new people, and let your child do what you've spent your life preparing him or her for—bouncing out of the home to flourish.

You may still have blue periods when you feel overcome by the loss of a young adult/child who was your companion. So, reduce your anxiety by tending to yourself. Look after your appearance and state of mind. Decide what you want to do: "I want to see funny movies. I want to go dancing with friends. I want to walk two miles every morning."

You're having anxiety attacks because your grown daughter is in a destructive relationship

This is a heartbreaker, indeed. In fact, some parents are so distressed by this kind of situation that they get depressed, making them less helpful as a support system. What's mind-boggling is realizing that you can no longer shield your kid from hurt and injury. This has been your life—and you got pretty darn good at it. When she was a kid, you helped her handle all types of problems—from school bullies, to difficult courses, to philandering boyfriends.

But you have to observe a certain hands-off element when you're dealing with a grown child who is married or living with someone. One mother of a daughter married to an alcoholic tells of seeing misery...but she could also tell that the young woman wanted to shield her family from the awful truth of what was going on. The mom was frustrated, but at least her daughter offered some reassurance: "If I need your help, you'll be the first person I'll call, Mom."

So, what happens if you see the situation endangering her health—mental or physical? In that case, forget about invisible barriers, and charge right in. Find a way to get her out. All too often, a person who's being abused feels helpless and worthless because cruelty eats away at self-esteem. She may need a wakeup call: "Honey, I'll pay your first month's rent and deposit on an apartment if you want to leave him—he's mistreating you."

If you're reluctant to interfere, remember that an abusive situation is no time to stand by quietly. On the other hand, if she wants codependency or total control, the choice is hers, not yours—as long as she's an adult and no children are being hurt.

So, how do you grit your teeth and bear it when you see signs of a destructive relationship...but your child doesn't want your help yet? By this point, you're probably thinking of her predicament all day and even waking up during the night worried. Try some of these ways of reducing your own anxiety:

- Anytime you start borrowing trouble—anticipating what you fear will happen—focus on today, and what's happening now.

- Review the facts. You don't think your daughter is happy. You think her husband is leaning on her financially and demeaning her personally. But you have to look at her point of view. She tells you that you're wrong—she doesn't mind supporting him, and she can handle his rudeness. Obviously, you don't see her marriage the way she does.

- Self-talk yourself down from high-anxiety: "I have felt this way before, and said so, and yet she still stays with him. I have to realize that this is her life, not mine. I can't make her choices."

- Do the worst-case-scenario exercise. Assuming that you truly don't think there's a risk of physical abuse, probably the worst thing that can happen is that they will end up divorced and she'll get hurt. Imagine what your role would be: "I'd help her get through it. I would be her confidante, help her realize that she can live without this man. I'd give her financial support if she needed it."

- Defuse demons. When you start telling yourself that you'll go crazy if she stays in this destructive relationship, look at the statement literally. Will you go crazy? No. But you won't like it. You'll tolerate the strain, and try to minimize it so that it's not on your mind all the time. Tell yourself: "I don't want her marriage at the forefront of my mind every day. I'd like to be a positive, happy part of her life. This is her life, and I can't run it, as much as I'd like to."

Your child is getting a divorce, which makes you anxious because your child is sad and hurt

You want to hold your child. You want to be protective. You even may wish to handle the arrangements and, if necessary, put out a contract on the ex.

But stop yourself. Now.

Find out what she wants from you. Don't make yourself a pain at a time when she has enough problems. You need to be steady and supportive, not volatile and judgmental.

If she wants to talk, listen. But restrain your urge to say, "I told you so." And don't *ever* say, "You'll get through this because billions of couples split up." That provides no comfort at all.

A person's grief feels uniquely awful, and to lump it in with a heap of others is to minimize it. Instead of minimizing the pain, let your kid know that you can see that she is hurting, and you're ready to help. If you can babysit while she takes a weekend getaway, do so. If you can help set up an apartment and make arrangements for a car loan, do that. Try to keep her busy during the transition from marriage to singledom—go to the movies, shop, cook together. Encourage her to find peace before dating again.

If neither your child nor her spouse wants counseling and everyone has agreed the relationship is over, suggest seeing a counselor anyhow. Most people are not as well as they think they are during periods of upheaval. Suggest that a few hours of therapy may help her get through the ordeal in a healthier way. Also, some time spent dissecting the old relationship will help form better future bonds.

Stay out of the fray, and work on rebuilding your child's self-esteem. Choosing the wrong partner doesn't have to be viewed as a "failure." It happens—as a matter of fact, about 50 percent of the time, it happens. People hook up with the wrong people, and later go their separate ways when things don't work out.

You're experiencing anxiety in your new role as a stepparent

"I'm not replacing your mother. I want to be a new friend."

The preceding phrase is a good mantra for stepparenting. But don't expect to do the blended-family transition without being rocked by anxiety. The Brady Bunch was great fun, but mostly fantasy. Unless you're the most serene person on the face of the earth, you'll experience a range of emotions and some high stress.

As the stepparent (and adult), try to handle the adjustment period without panic and without taking it out on your new stepchildren. Maybe you'll feel guilty when you realize that you look at your husband's children as objectively as a person who just walked in off the street. You don't feel that "all-forgiving veil" that comes with being a natural parent. That's okay. You'll probably develop empathy eventually.

Also, you may get tons of negativity from children who hate the idea of their father or mother remarrying. The fact that they're not rolling out the welcome mat should come as no surprise. Take their balking in stride. Kids have normal, natural feelings. Let them hold you at arm's length until they decide to accept the marriage. *You* have to be the adult. Don't get into shouting matches and don't guilt-trip them for not liking you. That will only increase your anxiety (they'll give you even more flak if you make them feel "naughty" for not wanting a stepparent).

Their nastiness will pass after they notice your loving, accepting, and friendly ways. Meanwhile, use the following tactics for positive stepparenting:

- Soft-sell your new role. If you're gentle, but assertive, in your approach, you're more likely to win compliance. Take the role of a "kind new friend." Don't come across as the devil's second in command.
- Let your mate be the "Bad Cop." Don't try to discipline early in the game. Wait until the relationship is well established. Until then, leave disciplinary tasks to your mate, who is a pro with these kids in that arena.

- Use top-notch communication skills. If you get nothing in return but name-calling, groans, and eye-rolling, that's okay. Back off and wait for a better day. If the kids are brutal toward you, say, "Can I tell you how I'm feeling about your reaction to having me in the family?"

  Most kids will at least let you talk. Say that you feel hurt because they don't seem to want to give you a chance. But add that you know things will improve. "Remember, I just want to be another supporter. Who can't use one more?"

- Break the pattern of negative thoughts spiraling out of control. One bad thought can lead to another, ramping up your panic level. Get a feel for what's *really* going on. Just because your new mate's kids are hitting you left and right with coldness doesn't mean they'll hate you forever. Don't take it to heart.

- Alter your panicky perception. Here's an example: "I know the next time that kid talks back to me, I'm going to explode." Acknowledge that you feel bad, but switch your response. You'll want to explode, but instead, you'll stay calm. Tell yourself: "The kid's going through a hard time and is not adjusting very well. This is about the child. I'll stay optimistic. One day, we'll have a great relationship. And if that doesn't happen, that's okay, too. I won't turn this standoff into a disaster."

- Train yourself not to let words pop out. Step back, think about how happy you'll be when things improve. Even if your stepchild is pummeling you with spitefulness, don't join in. Let it roll off your back.

- *Do* take a firm stand if your stepchild screams or curses. Simply say, "We don't scream in our home and we don't use profanity here. I'd rather talk to you when you feel like you can be respectful again." Don't get into it with the child. Buying into your stepchild's fury won't help your anxiety level, nor will it defuse the situation.

- Be patient. Kill your stepkids with kindness. Sooner or later, they'll realize you didn't marry their mom or dad just to be hateful to them. They'll go on to other vendettas, and you'll be a "thing" they'll get used to. Never forget children's basic selfishness; a few bribes (small gifts, chocolate bars, home-made cookies) won't hurt your popularity.

You're feeling anxious about your teen's casual attitude toward sex

You've got to get real when dealing with a teenager's sexuality issues. Denial won't work and demands are useless. And don't be surprised to feel your blood boiling when you get a sample of your kid's cavalier attitude. Remember, though, that teens like to sound saucier and more self-assured than they actually are. Posturing is cool in their world.

Meanwhile, over in "Anxietyville," you're battling natural worries about all the awful things that can happen to your teen—sexually transmitted diseases (STDs), pregnancy, date rape, among other nastiness. Truth is, you could feel anxiety throughout the teen years unless you find a lifeline right now. So, try these survival tips:

- Know what you can (and can't) do. In talking to your child about dating, relationships, and sex, get ready to listen. Don't set yourself up as a fountain of streaming advice.
- Underscore the gravity of making good decisions regarding sexual activity. Poor choices can be fatal. STDs, such as HIV and hepatitis, cannot be taken lightly.
- Promote good decision-making. Accept that you can't be there to hold your teen's hand during these turbulent years. But, you can be ready and willing to listen at any time, to anything, without passing judgment.
- Keep a cool head when your teen comes to you with a problem (big or small). As sweat breaks out in your armpits, self-talk: "I have handled a crisis before, and now my child wants me to help him handle a sex-crisis. I can do this."
- Be the adult. Treat sexual hurdles as your child's confrontations. You're there to facilitate and support. This isn't your life—your teen is growing up into an adult and has a say in what happens.

- Do discourage sexual activity in the teenage years. And share information on abstinence and on risks that come with sexual activity: STDs, date rape, pregnancy, and so forth. Equip your child with good information. Today, four of 10 American girls get pregnant at least once before they're out of their teens. And sexually transmitted diseases are proliferating wildly among U.S. high-school students. Statistics show that most teens have had sex by the time they graduate, and few of them opt for condoms or contraception of any kind. Teens indulge in oral sex in order to avoid pregnancy, and few know that STDs can also be transmitted via oral sex. Despite large-scale efforts of health agencies to educate young people, they remain fairly oblivious to the risks involved in unprotected sex—such as the fact that genital warts and genital herpes can be spread despite condom use. What you, as a parent, must do is provide guidance and information for your teen. Encourage abstinence or safe sex, whichever applies. If your daughter is sexually active, don't be in denial. She needs some form of birth control, and she should have an annual pap smear and be tested for HIV, chlamydia, and gonorrhea. Your son needs tests for STDs, too.

You obsess about your child's safety at school

We've seen countless horrors unfold on television. The bizarre shootings and bullying in schools are enough to make even a calm parent turn obsessive. If you have a tendency to be a worrier, you're probably "borrowing" huge amounts of misery each time you send your child off to school.

What can you do when you panic because you know you can't make your child's school 100-percent safe? Turn to anxiety-reducing techniques and coping skills, such as self-talk and thought-stopping (see Chapter 3). Do what you can do to improve safety, but be realistic about your inability to control fate.

Take practical steps to protect your children. Young kids should always be under adult supervision. Meet your school-age kids at the bus stop, or drop off and pick up your child from school.

You experience a great deal of anxiety from your child's long-term illness/disability

Feeling anxious about handling a child with a disability or long-term illness is certainly a normal reaction. Many parents have frequent worries about how to integrate such a child into the family—and how to make sure the child has a good life.

Some folks, dismayed by gloomy prospects, experience self-doubt, guilt, and distress. A randomized trial of community-based support for families of children with chronic illnesses reported in the *Archives of Pediatrics & Adolescent Medicine* (July 2001) showed that parents of these children are at high risk for secondary mental health problems, such as anxiety and depression. But, the anxiety levels of the 193 mothers in this trial decreased as a result of 15 months' interaction with the "Family-to-Family Network," where mothers of school-age kids with selected chronic illness were linked with mothers of older children with the same condition. Telephone contact, face-to-face visits, and family events led to improved mental health, especially in those with high baseline anxiety and moms who were themselves in poor health.

The isolation of long-term care can cause a great deal of anxiety. A parent may feel an extreme push-pull—resenting what is going on and wanting to care for the child to make life better. And the strain and responsibility aren't relieved by the transfer of a disabled child to a care facility.

You need to work for a balance between meeting the needs of the rest of the family and giving long-term care to your disabled child. You, as a parent, must find ways to cope with anxiety and worry. Insomnia, restlessness, mood swings, and reduced concentration will not help you deal with your child more effectively.

The following are some tips for caregivers and parents of a disabled child:

Use thought-stopping (Chapter 3). Manage your thoughts of dread by facing them. Consider reality versus your fears. Study your negative thoughts, and try to break out of the negative cycle. When you know that one thought is leading to another destructive one, snap yourself out of the haze of self-recrimination and sorrow. You can douse a thought. You see the sparks or flames of a scenario you've visited before, but this time, you're going to throw cold water on it. Stop it! The next time you feel the same string of thoughts lining up to stroll down your synapses, take yourself through the same routine: Stop!

An example: "I just know that my child is going to have an awful life, deprived of things other kids get to do…and this will make the whole family despondent, and detract from having a normal way of life." Snap out of it. No! You won't let that happen.

Instead, replace the thought: "I'm thankful that my child is alive and with us and enjoys life. We take good care of our children, but naturally, there are times when we feel frustrated and overloaded with responsibility. That's just going to happen. But as a parent, I can still be upbeat and have fun with my family."

Self-talk builds up your courage. Negative self-talk does the opposite.

You worry about your failures as a parent, or you're accused of being unloving and critical

No one gets everything right as a parent, but many of us do make a hobby of beating ourselves up about mistakes. Even though heavy-duty regret is a total waste of time, we still get out the list of things we didn't do and strap on loads of guilt if we see any hint of neurosis in our kids.

On the other hand, a parent who actually is unloving and critical needs some improvements as soon as possible—the younger your child, the more urgent this situation is.

The following are ideas for lessening your guilt about parenting slips and failures—when most of what you've done as a parent has been positive:

- Wake up daily with a positive mantra: "I am glad to have this day to embrace. I'll do my best to be a good person and parent, but I will not spend time rerunning past mistakes. I can do something about today only—and tomorrow."

- Conjure up a calming imagery: a beach with waves bathing your toes, the sound of rushing water soothing your mind, the sun rays warming your skin in a wonderful way. Take a mental hiatus—go there when the going gets rough. Don't fire back at your child with his or her failures. And don't buy into the guilt he tries to load on you. Express your love and say that you're listening. "I will try to be a good parent, so I hope you'll try to be a respectful kid."
- Watch the change in your own emotions. Shift the anxiety out of your life, and replace it with soothing feelings. If your child is still working to push your buttons, say, "I don't want to feel irritated or annoyed; I choose not to. I hope you'll learn to reduce your anger."

• • •

The parent who is distant, critical, and unloving faces a different scenario altogether. If your child shudders at the sight of you because you're a constant source of criticism, take a look at what you're doing. Try to make changes. How can you do better? Here are some guidelines:

- Discontinue the negative messages. If your reaction to your child's deeds in the past was to critique, carp, and lash out, use thought-stopping—and mouth-stopping—each time you start to do that again. Yes, you need to keep him out of danger, but no, it's not your job to spend all your waking hours "shaping up" your kid's coloring, clothes, eating, running, or jumping.
- Use a physical stopping method when you open your mouth to return to your old critical ways. Perhaps, you need to make a small badge to wear around the house that has the words "give good stuff" or "stop the madness." Whatever it takes, use a reminder so that you're constantly telling yourself that your new script calls for positives and not a string of critiques.
- Look for opportunities to praise. Find ways to let your child know you truly do love and appreciate him or her. If your daughter is drawing a picture, look at it and admire the colors she has chosen. If your son is making his bed, applaud a good effort.

- Express your pleasure that your child is alive. When you see your daughter, say how happy it makes you just to see her sweet face each day. Say "How lucky I am to have such a sweet daughter!"
- Give unexpected "drive-by" affection. Touch your son's hair fondly. Pat his shoulder. Kiss him and hug him.
- Keep the good stuff coming. You can undo the damage you have done in the months (years) when you were failing as a parent.

You feel extreme anxiety because your child is cruel to animals

If your child is cruel to animals, you're looking at something that should raise great concern. In 1905, Sigmund Freud urged doctors to pay special attention to children who were cruel to animals. The FBI and researchers have linked animal cruelty to domestic violence, child abuse, serial killings, and killings by school-age children. In 1999, five of six U.S. students who went on shooting rampages had histories of animal cruelties in their childhoods.

The general feeling among mental-health professionals is that animal abuse is a sign of two things: a deeply disturbed family as well as a personality flaw in the abuser. Not surprisingly, children who see their parents reacting to anger with violence are often going to respond by battering the next most vulnerable family member below them, often a pet. Studies also show that animal-abusing kids are usually child-abuse victims.

In an article by the Orlando Humane Society, provided on the Internet by the American Humane Society, it was found that in a study of males in jail for violent crimes, 25 percent of the criminals reported "substantial cruelty" to animals during their young years. This was compared with a control group of free, nonviolent individuals, none of whom were cruel to animals.

The Society for the Prevention of Cruelty to Animals reports that in a study of 57 familes being treated for child abuse, 88 percent had abused animals *(www.ohs-spca.org/violence.htm)*. In two-thirds of cases, the abusive parent had killed or injured animals as a form of controlling a child; but in one-third, the kids had used the animals as scapegoats for their anger.

Confront this problem head on. Lead your child to counseling and intervention. Professional help is pivotal in this serious form of aggressive and hostile behavior.

You're worried because your 12-year-old seems anxious about everything

Parents can do a great deal to improve the life of a child who seems to have been born with a tendency to feel anxious about developmental hurdles and social encounters. Some of the measures that can help are the following:

- Try to make your child's life fairly predictable. Change sometimes upsets anxious children, so try not to give your youngster too many surprises.

- Let her know what's coming up—visitors, challenges, outings, whatever.

- Ask what you can do when you see signs of anxiety. Don't decide what you think she wants or "what would be good." Instead, find out what your kid could use help with. Talk and listen.

- Give praise when your child seems stymied by experiences but still manages to make baby steps. But don't go overboard, insisting this is the most wonderful thing that has ever happened—she will doubt your judgment.

- Don't always "fix things up." If you follow your child lifelong, you can probably make sure that she never, ever has to do anything that's hard. But when you're no longer around, your kid will be clueless.

- Offer encouragement when your child has to face a tough challenge, instead of facilitating the natural desire to skip the things that she feels anxious doing.

- When she gets anxious, stay calm and don't get agitated. (Naturally, you're concerned about your child's anxiety, but you shouldn't let it rule your life.)
- Maintain an attitude of acceptance, but don't act as if you feel sorry for your kid because of undue anxiousness. Often, people rise above such problems, especially when they have a strong supporter who reassures them that they can do things well.
- Offer tools for surmounting fears. When she says, "there's no way I can do that," say that it "feels" that way, but in fact, it can probably be done. Give ideas: "Breathe slowly and push away negative thoughts. What you're feeling is scary, all right, but you won't die or get hurt. You'll get a handle on this challenge at some point."

6

Fighting Panic Attacks in College

Anxiety-Busting Tools for This Chapter:
- Changing responses to cues.
- Improving social skills.
- Relationship-building.
- Effective expression of needs.

Big exams give you panic attacks

I<small>F EVER THERE WERE A CLASSIC CASE FOR NEEDING TO CHANGE YOUR</small> response to cues, this is it. You're probably overwhelmed by the power your professor has in testing you, so you imagine the test that's coming up as threatening and way too hard. You see your-self as a screwup, inadequate for the challenge. So, you expect failure and focus on how bad you are at that subject. But that's an approach you're going to bury now, because it's not working for you!

Instead, sample these ideas for calming your test anxiety by tak-ing a more positive approach:

- Look at a test as a chance to "show off" rather than a scary showdown.

- Figure out what it would take to get yourself into a state of preparedness that would allow you to feel like you were going to march into that classroom and score big.
- Think positively. List everything that you have to lose if you study hard, yet end up making a bad grade. Truthfully, you will have lost nothing but some time, and you'll get some practice in study skills.
- Give yourself one full-fledged high-energy study session preparing for your next exam. Pull out all the stops.
- The night before the exam, think tranquil thoughts when you take breaks from studying. If negative thoughts creep into your mind, run them off. Keep saying this: "I'll find out what I can do on this exam, and if I do fail it, no one dies."
- Eat a healthy breakfast before you go to the test. If you have time, do a few stretches and sit-ups, as if you're getting ready to go a few rounds with Evander Holyfield. (In addition, eating eggs the morning of a test will ramp your memory into high gear—try it!)
- When you get to the classroom, do some deep, slow breathing for a few minutes. Repeat this during the test if you feel panic rising. Look around you and smile silently, wishing goodwill to all of those gathered, including the instructor/professor.
- Do some self-talk when you think, "I can't do this—I'm too dumb to be in college!" Instead, tell yourself this: "I'm as smart as many of the people in this class, and I can do well on tests. If I don't make it happen this time, I'll find out what it takes to do better next time."
- Pace yourself. Make sure you don't get bogged down trying to answer a question you're unsure of and waste time that you could have spent on the ones you may know.
- Stay hopeful throughout. No matter how many questions you come across that you can't answer, stay the course. Tell yourself, "I'm sure I'll come to some things I know...."
- After your test, rate yourself on how well you handled your stress. Don't worry about your grade—that's a major waste of time now that it's done. Focus on positive thoughts. Stay distracted. Wonder what you'll have for dinner. Think about

how you didn't waste as much time as you may have in the past. Be good to yourself with praise if you did well with handling your anxiety.

You've moved into a dorm and are having trouble with this new independence

Moving away from the home that you grew up in can cause enormous upheaval. Some young people make the transition with ease, loving every minute of it. Others, however, find this a nauseating venture into the brave new world of decision-making. Some even have panic attacks.

And what happens when a parent sees his or her offspring having trouble with the transition? Some just hope that time will take care of everything. Others try to be proactive, jumping into the fray.

But the college kid with emotional distress may not willingly accept a parent's intervention. Sometimes, a young person will refuse attempts to help resolve the problem, show extreme irritability, or fly into a rage when confronted. A study reported in *Canadian Family Physician* (May 2001) by the Mood and Anxiety Disorders Clinic at British Columbia Children's Hospital found that about 10 percent of adolescents have anxiety disorders, with common spin-offs being class avoidance and substance abuse.

Although research has shown that medications can effectively help adults who have generalized anxiety, panic disorders, and social phobia, anxiety disorders in the young have drawn little research. Mental health professionals do believe they can help children by leading them to changing behavior and increased understanding of their panicky situations. And, even with limited data, doctors report good results in using selective serotonin reuptake inhibitors (SSRIs) to treat anxiety in children, according to a report in *Current Psychiatry Reports* (August 2001).

Developmental studies suggest that management of anxiety in youngsters should feature interventions to examine anxiety in parents. They should give parenting advice on behavior management and family-conflict resolution, as well as treatment of the child's difficulty that is specifically designed to decrease risk of depression.

The Journal of the American Academy of Child & Adolescent Psychiatry (July 2001) described a pilot study of school-based behavioral treatment for social anxiety disorder in adolescents. It said that researchers found that school environments are excellent settings for behavioral treatment, as that's where adolescents usually battle social phobia. When behavior treatment was applied to six adolescents with social anxiety disorder, the result was that half no longer met the diagnostic criteria for this phobia afterward. In other words, you can give kids some pointers and many will get the hang of it.

You're stressed because your child is pledging a Greek letter organization or playing sports

Most young adults don't do well under extreme pressure or exaggerated expectations from parents, teachers, or coaches. A kid who's involved in athletics (or the parent of one) should be on the lookout for signs of excessive pressure by coaches.

There should be a constant flow of feedback and information, athlete to parents to coaches, and around the loop again. Parents of kids who are getting pressured to meet certain expectations should monitor the situation carefully to make sure things don't get out of hand.

If you notice that a coach, a "pledge-master," a sorority member, or another "person in charge" is involved in "thought-dictating" (telling your child what he or she should feel or think), interrupt this negative exercise. Thought-dictating can lead to a real trap: Your impressionable child may begin to believe that the primary goal in the activity is to please everyone...at his or her expense. In truth, the goal should be enjoying the activity. Participating in a sport or club should be satisfying and contribute to personal growth, and you should explain to your child that the whole idea is to have fun.

In the case of a young athlete, a trained sports psychologist or counselor can be a good source of advice and support on areas such as anxiety control, motivation, and concentration. In examining special concerns of female figure skaters, a research report in *Clinical Sports Medicine* suggests the kind of traits that should be emphasized are honesty, respect, clarity, consistency, and sincerity.

Parents and coaches should watch for instances of kids being treated with sarcasm, ridicule, and disrespect by people in authority. If you see it, don't fail to express your displeasure immediately. Also, brief your child on her rights. Shabby treatment or comments should not be tolerated—even if someone insists that these are the rites-of-passage she must go through. In the case of sorority/fraternity hazing, let your child know that it's fine to have boundaries and to stick to them. Remind him of reports on fraternity hazing that led to chugalugging alcohol to the point of poisoning and death. These were kids caught up in peer-pleasing, afraid to complain that frat brothers were being outrageous.

You're having trouble with an instructor

Here, reality therapy comes in handy. Sure, you can suffer plenty of anxiety when you're forced to deal with an unreasonable teacher, but it's also true that in real life, you'll have difficult people riding roughshod over you at some time, whether that person is a boss, a teacher, or an opposing attorney during a deposition.

To adjust, you need a set of effective coping mechanisms such as the following:

- Admit to yourself that the mean-spirited treatment isn't normal and you hate it.

- Remember that there will be times in life when you can't escape being subjected to hateful people, so you must learn how to cope.

- Use self-talk. Tell yourself: "It's unconscionable for someone to treat me (or anyone else) this way, but I can handle it. I'm developing a tougher skin that lets me put this in perspective. Cruel, domineering people surely can't be very happy, so I'll give them my pity, not my fear. The bottom line is this: I will not let this person mess up my day!"

You're anxiety-ridden holding down a job while attending college

Knowing what you can and cannot do about this situation will help. Accept that there will be many times when you are exhausted, under-prepared for a class, and frustrated that you have a situation that seems rougher than that of a student who doesn't have to work. But this is what is. And your attitude, in reframing this in a doable context, will make the difference.

Try this self-talk script: "I don't have enough time to prepare for class and I don't like that. But I can still get as much out of my education as I possibly can. I do not have to make As to succeed; I need a degree and I'll get a degree. I won't beat myself up about my situation, but I'll make the most of college, as a big opportunity."

Here is an important skill to learn: Be happy about what is, not what you wish were the case.

You've started dating more and you feel conflicted about sex

Many young people experience sexual blooming in college. There are no parental constraints. There are more opportunities to be alone with the opposite sex. And attached to that is an influx of confusing messages about what the whole thing should really mean.

We all want to love and to be loved. This is universal. But sex, in itself, isn't love. You will soon learn that many people just regard sex as a form of mindless, exploitative recreation. Some young people are comfortable with this. Others, who have higher expectations of "love" and place higher value on themselves, want something more than what the animals in the field are doing.

Understanding the sexual arena baffles many of us, and the quandary often continues for decades. For that reason, you'd be smart to set up your approach to sexuality early on.

Ask yourself a few questions: Do you want to remain chaste? Do you want sex as a part of a loving, enduring relationship, or are you out for some casual sex? These questions can produce huge anxiety in young people, both male and female. And most worthy counselors would tell young people to proceed with caution: In the shark-infested waters of early sexuality, you'll find crass exploitation and sexually transmitted diseases that can alter the course of your entire life. Although movies, such as *American Pie,* give the impression that sex is little more than a lark, ask someone who ends up with genital herpes how much fun comes with having painful lesions, not to mention having to experience rejection. These aren't lightweight issues.

You can't stick your head in the sand and pretend that you are immune or that you won't be devastated if this happens to you. By far, the smart way to go is an eyes-wide-open, self-preserving attitude. Don't think that you can win someone's love by giving him or her sex; it doesn't work that way. And no one wants to be used. Do believe that you have to look out for yourself, especially in the self-centered universe of high school and college, when few young people can see beyond their own fulfillment.

Keep reminding yourself that you value your sexuality and want it to be part of a loving experience. You should not have to feel frustrated thinking, "Why won't that creep I had sex with call me?"

You feel tremendous anxiety as a college freshman who can't get a date

The swirling social atmosphere of college can make a person who lacks strong social skills feel bewildered and unwanted. But you can find your way out of this misery by determining what you want in your social life, and how you want it, and what it takes to get there.

Let's assume that you're so into your studies that you'd be perfectly satisfied with dating occasionally. You want nothing heavy, perhaps—just some getting out and meeting people.

You need to show that you're interested in other people. Ask questions about their lives. This is how you make friends.

You can even make yourself madly dateable. First, figure out what's holding you back. If you're painfully shy, find a hobby club or religious group in which you can slowly make friends and develop your meeting-and-greeting skills.

If you think your appearance is the drawback, why do you think so? If you look around on campus, you'll see that there is someone for everyone; college isn't just a dating world for beautiful people. However, you can also do some honest self-scrutiny. Are you tipping the scales at 30 pounds over what's healthy for your height? If so, lose weight to get healthier, and the "better look" will be a side benefit.

Is your style in need of tweaking? Go to a chic salon to have their personnel do a makeover on you. We aren't talking vanity—it's more like survival in a looks-oriented jungle. If you can't afford a professional makeover, you can pick up all kinds of good ideas from the magazines *InStyle* and *Allure*, both of which have special makeover issues and great tips year-round.

If you're a parent, don't bother telling your teen or grown kid, "you want someone to love you for *you*, so who cares what's on MTV?" You're missing the point. No one can love your child for his or her sweet self if it's hard to get past the appearance.

Help your child deal with the real world. If she would be happier if she were dating and knowing more people, and all it takes is a little makeup or a cooler pair of shoes, why not try it? You're just opting for some "packaging" that paves the way to new friendships. Then, your child will get a chance to show off her intelligence, charm, and sweetness. Also, encourage your child to work on her social skills (see Chapter 3 for tips on improving social skills and relationship-building).

You had panic attacks and dropped out of school; now you feel despair

College can be overwhelming—and for some, it constitutes culture shock. Perhaps, the fact that you dropped out—to step back and reevaluate what went wrong—will help to ensure you greater success the next time around, if you decide to tackle school again.

You may have intense feelings of terror that strike suddenly, and you can't predict when another attack will occur. In between, you worry about the same panicky spiral happening again. Panic attack symptoms include chest pain, flushes or chills, pounding heart, nausea, lightheaded feeling, shaking, shortness of breath, fear of dying, sweating, and a feeling of losing your mind. (See Chapter 1 to examine in greater detail.) You may feel this way for a couple of minutes, eight minutes, or even longer.

You definitely need to seek treatment if your disorder has become disabling. It can lead to depression, drug or alcohol dependence, and/or phobias. But very often, early treatment can keep panic attacks from progressing into more pervasive problems.

Most people who have panic attacks can learn ways to change their behaviors, some need medication, and some need a combination of behavior change and drug therapy. You learn how to view your panic situations differently, which may mean slowly exposing yourself to the things you fear in order to become desensitized to them.

Some medications prevent panic attacks or reduce their frequency and severity. Two that are effective are benzodiazepines and antidepressants. (For more on fine-tuning your coping skills, see Chapter 3.)

7

Handling Couple Troubles That Cause Anxiety

Anxiety-Busting Tools for This Chapter:

- Changing responses to cues.
- Relationship-building.
- Anger management.
- Learning to avoid blame-shifting.
- Thought-stopping.

Your live-in lover refuses to get married

A 38-YEAR-OLD WOMAN WONDERED IF SHE WAS HAVING CHRONIC PMS, or if her anxiety, mood swings, and overwhelming fatigue were symptoms of severe emotional stress. Anna* had read enough health articles to know that imbalances of hormones can cause PMS-like symptoms, but she also knew that she was upset because she and her live-in boyfriend of five years, who were once a very loving couple, were now unhappy. She was anxious and depressed most of the time. Her psychiatrist put her on Paxil, which helped temporarily. However, after a few months, she hated the side effects—dry mouth, constipation, drowsiness, and sometimes, anxiety!

Anna's key issue was that her live-in boyfriend didn't want to get married...and she did. They had discussed this many times, and he hadn't budged. Thus, she always switched on a negative mood anytime the subject came up. Ready to hate her partner's negativity, she cranked up her pity meter, which started ticking the minute they got "The Big Issue" out on the table. She wanted to improve her situation. Continued use of medication was only a patch.

To resolve her anxiety, she knew step one was defining the problem: "What bothers you about the situation you're in and why do you think it causes you anxiety?"

Anna's answers were:

1. Several of my friends have recently gotten married, and I wonder why their lovers think they're special enough to marry— and mine doesn't. There must be something wrong with me.
2. My boyfriend says he doesn't want to get married because of his two disastrous experiences with marriage, but I think this is just a lame excuse.
3. My life is in limbo. I have a boyfriend; I'm waiting for him to ask me to marry him.
4. I stay mad at him. I think he is being mean and pig-headed, and that if he really loved me, we'd be making wedding plans.
5. When we discuss the matter, I attack and say, "I've done this and that for you...." Then, for days, we avoid each other.
6. I have lost all my joy. I have suicidal thoughts. I feel worthless because I cannot inspire this man to want to marry me.

Next, Anna addresses the statements above by sorting logical and illogical thoughts, and here's what she discovered about her situation:

You made assumptions based on nothing other than that a man was in love with you. Because you believe love leads to marriage, you thought this relationship would lead to marriage. You set up a cohabiting situation that wasn't what you wanted at all. You chose a mate you enjoy being with, and that's a good thing. But you entered into a serious liaison (living together) without clarifying in advance your goals for this relationship.

Probably, his refusal to marry is no reflection on you whatsoever. You're the same bright, attractive woman you were before you met him—and you will be the same after you and he are no longer together. The reality is, he doesn't want to get married, and you do.

Still, you refuse to believe he is all that afraid of marriage just because of his marital disasters. But why would he fabricate this reason? He's possibly telling the truth as he knows it. The fear and loathing he has attached to the institution is real to him. Accept that being marriage phobic is his problem. But its huge effect on your life is your problem. Your life is in limbo, but you can't shift your blame because your partner has never changed his premise at all. You can accept living together, you can leave, or you can ask him to leave. No one's making you stay in a relationship that screams "dead-end" to you. You can make a decision and live with the results.

Slowly, Anna realizes something *must* change. The relationship has deteriorated, and she knows that her inability to accept his goals for the relationship (status quo) versus hers (marriage) spells incompatibility. Being at odds with a loved one is stressful and depressing.

A woman in this situation must face a few critical points: First, you cannot *make* him want to get married. You can't tell him what to do even though you'd love to. Second, one thing you can do is change the destructive pattern you have going nowadays, and replace it with one that's more positive, more change-inducing, and less offensive. If you suddenly acted upbeat and peaceful with yourself, he'd be less apt to rebel. Perhaps, the two of you could even rediscover what you liked about each other. Why keep rerunning flawed scripts and expect them to work, magically, this particular time?

Being happy with yourself will help you find closure. What you have with your partner isn't working. Say it. *Believe it.* Face what can and cannot happen. Instead of blaming and blaming again, take care of someone whose behavior you do have a say in—and that's you. You haven't inched things forward one bit by engaging your partner harshly and making demands. You aren't closer to him in any way.

Realize when you've reached the wretched point of entertaining thoughts of suicide, as you mentioned, you **must seek help** for your depression and anxiety—and do what you can to break this unproductive pattern.

Try these anxiety-curbing techniques when you feel that stress is escalating:

- Let an auditory signal rewire you. When you're about to blow a gasket, use castanets or a New Year's noisemaker to signal "stop." You then step back and take a deep breath.
- Try using a visual cue: Imagine a billboard flashing in front of you, reminding you to think about what's really happening, its ultimate outcome, and the way you would successfully endure that.

Using an auditory or visual stimulus may be effective in breaking the cycle in your brain.

You're experiencing anxiety because your mate is addicted to Internet porn

Fraught with worry and anxiety, 47-year-old Rosalie* reported having migraines and dizzy spells. She had gotten married a year ago—her second marriage, after being single for 10 years. Things seemed great. Her husband told her often he loved being married to her.

Then he began to spend most evenings away from her, alone with his computer in his study. One night she walked into his study, and he hit the key to close the screen, as if he were hiding something. Eventually, she found out that he was watching Internet porn.

When he wasn't at work, he was glued to porn sites and steamy chat rooms. When she told him she hated what he was doing, he told her she was being ridiculous—that this was just like looking at *Playboy* and all men did it.

To Rosalie, cybersex felt like cheating. Her anxious feelings didn't stop, and her husband didn't stop either. Rosalie's chest hurt, and it was sometimes hard to breathe. A friend told her that Internet addiction is epidemic...and that at least her husband wasn't *really* cheating. Rosalie believed that sooner or later, one woman in a sexually charged chat room, or an e-mail relationship, would try to arrange a meeting.

The following are some tips for problem-solving that are right for Rosalie, or for someone in her situation:

- Don't take the standoff personally. Avoid the natural tendency to personalize the situation by blaming yourself. "If only I'd been prettier, he wouldn't have resorted to the Internet." Don't do it. Admit that you have a problem, that you want something to change, but you have a right to want a healthier relationship—one in which your husband focuses on you.

- Send irrational thoughts away. These include: "I should blame myself because if he were happy with me, he wouldn't need to look elsewhere for stimulation," "He turned away from me because I'm getting old, and I don't look great like the porn chicks," or "I bet he thinks I'm a dud in bed."

- Look at your husband's hobby as his problem (or fixation), not yours. Maybe he'd still be downloading porn if Julia Roberts were lying in his bed. Perhaps, he's an Internet porn addict who has an easier time relating to fantasy than reality—women who are three-dimensional, complete with minds, and hearts, and personalities.

- Challenge his argument that you're the cause and that "all men do it." Redirect the confrontation back on track. Find out whether your mate is willing to change a destructive habit—one that's rotting the fabric of your marriage.

For your discussion with him, try using these assertiveness thoughts:

- I'll go into the discussion with conviction that I have the right to tell him what I want and need.
- Saying how I feel and asking for what I want are not selfish things.
- I'm not going to worry about whether my expression of thoughts that conflict with those of someone else will result in separation, or rejection.
- Expressing what concerns me doesn't amount to imposing on him.

- I'll start out assuming that my mate, by having expressed love for me, is also saying he cares what I think and how his deeds and words affect me.
- I won't expect him to read my mind. He'll know what I'm thinking only after I've shared the information.
- I expect to be treated with respect. His listening to how I feel about things is a critical part of that.
- I'll say what I think, but if my mate says he doesn't care what I think or can't respond to what I need, I'll take the steps necessary to take care of myself.
- I won't belittle my mate's feelings or beliefs, nor will I accept his making mincemeat of my feelings and beliefs.

• • •

Next comes dealing with the aftermath of confronting someone with information he doesn't want to hear. The worst you'll face will come from taking a stand that annoys your mate. Hopefully, you'll find that he, too, values the relationship, and the two of you will come up with a new and improved script for your marriage.

Perhaps you and your mate would benefit from a frank discussion of your sex life and your needs in that regard. (See tips on sexual performance later in this chapter.) Seek counseling from a minister, priest, marriage counselor, or therapist, and find out what can be done to improve your relationship.

You feel extreme anxiety about your mate's shopping addiction

A mate who has compulsive addictions can be a handful. So, you worry. And worry that lasts for months can signal generalized anxiety disorder (GAD). If your mate's shopping addiction makes you feel irritable, tense, restless, tired, and you have difficulty focusing on tasks, you could have GAD—especially if your worrying has spanned several months.

Managing anxiety can mean simply reframing the matter so that you can get your arms around it. Promise yourself that you'll tell your mate how these actions are affecting you. Explain in advance that each of you gets 15 minutes to talk uninterrupted while the other listens, and see if your mate is agreeable to that plan. Explain that because you are married, overspending impacts you, and you think that compulsive shopping might point to "issues" that need to be resolved.

Many people think that enough "things" will bring happiness. But when splurges don't fill that emotional "hole," they bounce back and forth from buying sprees to buyer's remorse.

After you express yourself to your mate, look at the reality of what you can and can't do. "I can't make my partner stop shopping compulsively. But I can decide what my responses will be."

Depending on the financial situation of your family, you have to decide if this is a huge issue (a potential deal-breaker), a minor annoyance, or somewhere in between.

Case in point: A multimillionaire hated his wife's produce-buying habits. She bought crates of fruit at a farmers' market, and sometimes the family failed to eat all of the bananas or apples, and the fruit spoiled. The sight set him off, and he'd try to make his wife feel guilty, but she continued to buy her large quantities of produce.

Obviously, the issue wasn't 20 dollars; this couple could afford a few crates of fruit. The issue was this: the guy didn't think she cared, and it irked him. That lack of communication carried over into other parts of their marriage: kids, vacations, sex, and others. Soon, he was convinced that he was just a "free lunch" to her, and he moved out. Six months later they were divorced.

At any rate, whether your partner is ridiculously extravagant, or minimally wasteful, you want to be heard. But don't expect to dictate the other person's decisions. Being married to someone doesn't make you that person's boss or decision-maker.

What you can do is toss the problem off your lap. Either your mate will or won't stop shopping madly. But you can change your attitude: "This is not my problem. I won't mess up my life by continuing to obsess about this. If it becomes a deal-killer, I'll know. And then my choices are counseling, staying, or leaving."

Your mate's nagging gives you anxiety attacks

So, what happens when someone lives with a nag? Whether child or mate, the person being hit with the rat-a-tat-tat of failings sees the nagger coming, and makes an attempt to escape. The fight-or-flight response kicks in immediately when you have a nagging spouse. You're accused of trying to get away from the criticism that "someone" thinks you so richly deserve.

How do you rid yourself of this source of massive anxiety? Simple. You insist on being treated with respect. And, someone who nags you night and day is not treating you respectfully.

Change the dynamics. Ask when you can sit down with your mate. When you do get some quiet time, describe how this treatment makes you feel. When your partner responds, listen carefully and don't interrupt. Make eye contact, and repeat what is said by the nagger: "So you're saying you always end up nagging because I'm messed up in so many ways that you're trying to fix me."

Surely, you can admit that you have failings. But don't agree that part of a mate's "job description" is shaping up the other person. Ask your spouse to think about this—the idea that when people get married, they accept each other "as is." Tell your spouse that you will agree to work on things that are bothersome. If your mate calls your concerns exaggerated or unfounded, point out that you would not be discussing them if the situation were working.

During this sharing, measure the anxiety you are experiencing. On a scale of one to 10, how does it feel? Moderate your reactions by taking slow, deep breaths. Tell yourself: "I'll stay calm because I love my mate and want to work things out."

Remind yourself that it's normal to feel tense during a "couple trouble" talk. But if you can keep a level head, you'll come closer to making progress.

Don't call up old past baggage—things your mate has done that annoyed you; stay in the moment. You want to make some strides toward a more respectful relationship right here, right now. If things grow heated, try saying one of the following to yourself:

- This is a bit unpleasant, but I can handle it.

- I'll get past these anxious feelings.
- Anxiety is not unbearable. I won't make something minor into something major.

You worry about your inability to meet your mate's expectations

This problem can be one of distorted perception. (Or not.)

Perhaps, you're making your mate's expectations larger than life in your mind, mainly because pleasing him or her is very important. Ask yourself: "Does it really matter greatly to my mate whether I'm meeting this expectation, or am I projecting my belief that it matters a lot?"

If you're not sure what the answer is, ask. If it involves money, ask, "Is it my imagination, or is my low salary really driving you crazy with disappointment at my performance?"

Let's say the answer is "You're just a worrier. It's your job and your business whether you get a raise or not." Okay, that means your perception is wrong. The truth is, you feel unhappy with yourself, and so you're assuming—by projecting—that your mate shares this disappointment.

On the other hand, what if you're right? Your mate expresses disappointment and thinks you're a slug. To decrease your anxiety, jot down a list of what you think might happen (worst-case scenario) if you insist that the nagging ends.

Hypothetically, you might list:

1. I may be alone if I refuse to be beaten up verbally.
2. I'll freak if my mate gets upset.
3. I'll be alone if I get divorced.
4. No one will want a loser like me.
5. I'll never be happy alone.
6. I feel like such a dork for having anxiety attacks just because my mate thinks I'm incompetent at my job.

Now, go down your list and point out (to yourself) the holes in each idea:

1. Would it be so bad if you were alone? After all, you're miserable. On the other hand, if you insist on respectful treatment, your mate might have higher regard for you, which will improve your self-image.
2. So what if you freak when your mate gets upset? That's all right.
3. Will you really be alone? Do you honestly think there is only one person in the entire world who would want to be around you?
4. This one can't be true because your premise is that you're not a loser—and you don't want to be treated like one. Your expectations for yourself should be at the forefront of your mind. Satisfy yourself that you are working hard. Perhaps getting ahead is not important to you. If you want a raise, figure out what it would take to make that a reality.
5. Being without this person is not a catastrophe. Being unhappy is just that—being unhappy. It happens. You will be happy again if you want to be happy again.
6. Experiencing anxiety in stressful situations shouldn't make you feel like an oddball. It's normal. What's important is learning how to cope with uncomfortable feelings.

You obsess about your mate's growing discontent, and you're afraid he will leave you

If fears of abandonment are plaguing you and nothing can be said to make things better, try positive self-talk. Repeat this each time you experience thoughts that lead to panic attacks.

For example, if you can handle the worst-possible scenario—that you're right and your mate is going to leave you—then you probably can get through that and anything short of that, right? So, devise a script that will lead you through the tough times. Let's say you go home one day and your mate has done the cowardly thing of moving out while you were gone. You find a note: "I love you but I can't live with you." You'll feel distraught, all right, but guess what? You'll make it.

In fact, you can have some "lines" ready that are going to help you cope with that anxiety-provoking situation, and others. Consider the following to jumpstart your thinking:

- I will not die, get sick, or quit work if my mate leaves.
- Worrying in advance about something that does not happen is a waste of my time.
- I'll stay in control and think about alternatives for living happily and by myself.
- I'll concentrate on what I need to do.
- I'll use a word to calm me down when my emotions start flailing around. "Chill" will be my keyword.
- If I begin to feel breathless or feel my heart palpitating, I will sit down and breathe deeply. I'll fix myself a glass of hot tea and a piece of cinnamon toast.
- I will admit to myself that these are not the best of times, but I'll remember that I have weathered rough things in the past.
- I will reassure myself that I do have the ability to calm myself by calling up my Sun Scene (see the 30-day plan in Chapter 4).
- I feel very anxious, but that doesn't make me a misfit. It just makes me human.
- I will tell myself "good going!" when I get through the event without having a "panic episode."
- When the day is over, I'll pat myself on the back for having dealt with the situation. I'll remember how I handled this so that can help me the next time I'm frightened.
- I'll remind myself there are better times ahead, and I'll stay upbeat about the possibility of making other friends and finding someone who suits me better.

You feel huge anxiety because your mate is nasty-tempered and often lashes out at you

You need to understand that you aren't going to alter a person's basic temperament. Perhaps, this was a trait that wasn't unveiled until after marriage, which makes it even more difficult. Or maybe you knew about it but believed you could live with it. Clarify what you can handle by first writing down some of your fears:

- When my mate screams and has a tantrum, I think I will be hit and perhaps killed.
- Being at odds with someone I love causes me huge anxiety.
- I wonder how I could be such a mess that I cause these fits of temper.

Now, examine each statement. Is the first one of these based on reality—were you hit? Or is it fiction that you have conjured up because you have never dealt with an ill-tempered individual? If you have been hurt, get out of the house, seek counseling, and go from there. Physical and mental abuse is one totally legitimate reason for leaving a marriage.

Second, can you learn to accept being at odds with your mate? Maybe that isn't as awful as you think it is. Not agreeing with a loved one is absolutely okay, but getting bombarded with insults and curses isn't. Set your boundaries and make these clear to your mate.

And finally, ask yourself how often in the past you have inspired fits of temper in others. If the answer is never, that should shed some light on the situation for you. This is your mate's problem. You're not causing temper fits. Your mate's inner turmoil is causing them, and you're the handy recipient of the wrath. Usually, angry people are really people who are hurting, so they lash out at those closest to them.

What should you do when your spouse has a temper tantrum? You can try the following:

- Walk out of the room while he goes ballistic.
- Leave the house and take a timeout.
- Say that you won't accept being treated disrespectfully just because your mate is feeling out of control.
- Look at these shenanigans as absurd behavior that you don't intend to submit yourself to; if your son was doing that, he would be sent to his room.
- You won't cower and you won't show your mate that you will be a punching bag.

Your live-in lover wants to get married, but you don't

Being at cross-purposes with a mate is one of the biggest and most common anxiety-provokers. Of course, two people never live in complete harmony all the time. But a key issue, such as marriage, is definitely something that will continue to be a problem, unless you resolve the issue once and for all.

First, look at your mate's point of view. She wants to get married, and you're saying you don't intend to deliver that, ever. So, the loving thing to do, in that case, is to be honest. Explain that the only logical route is going your separate ways because you don't want to hold your mate back from marrying.

The other possibility is reexamining your feelings about marriage. You hate the institution because of what it meant to you with an ex, but would things be different with this person? Maybe you're rushing to judgment.

The only other course of action is twisting your mate's arm to your point of view—that living together is fine—that you two are "married without the paper to prove it," and that your love should override society's needs.

What is key to reducing anxiety, though, is resolving this issue. Either defuse it, so that it's no longer a source of anxiety because you now agree or accept the inevitable: that two people with different views on what constitutes an everlasting relationship will not be able to stay together.

Don't live under stress and discomfort; this isn't a positive situation. Far too often, couples come to counseling with a huge amount of anxiety, wondering why they have allowed themselves to live in such a compromised way for so long. They feel cheated out of years of their lives, almost acting as if they'd never been right there in the house where they were free to speak up, and leave if they needed to.

Your mate's controlling nature fills you with anxiety

Dealing with a control freak requires assertiveness, and, ironically, that is the first trait that gets stomped out when a mate lords his power over you. You feel anxious, inept, and vulnerable to the whims of your beloved. Unfortunately, a controlling mate can be one of the most dangerous.

Occasionally, a teen boy manages to control his girlfriend because she's so eager to please. Perhaps, she had no father or an uninvolved one—and she believes she can "love away" the meanness in her boyfriend. In older couples, the same thing happens. A man falls in love with a woman who decides to fix him up, so she takes over his life.

What's the answer to destructive relationships? The bottom line is this: you can't let someone change your priorities, alter your basic self, and distance you from family and friends. If any one of these is happening to you, consider the following ways of changing things:

- Get help from a doctor or counselor. You need an objective "shoulder to cry on," and you may also need medication to help you get through your panic and/or anxiety.
- Tell your mate what you need—a less controlling attitude, less insistence on monopolizing all your time, whatever. Explain how the current situation makes you feel anxious and upset—and that you don't want to live this way.
- Ask your mate to mirror back to you a response that shows understanding. If he refuses to do this, note how unwilling he is being ("that's ridiculous—don't give me that psychobabble mumbo-jumbo!"). Do you want a lifelong partner who is totally self-absorbed and disinterested in your needs? If your mate responds in a positive way, give him time to show that he is willing to make some changes, and see if these can be put into place.
- Remove yourself from the unhealthy situation. A controlling mate is usually manipulative enough to convince you that "if you hadn't made me mad, I wouldn't have had to yell at you." This means you'll have a hard time coming to your senses, or

altering the dynamics, unless you put some miles between the two of you. If you're married, move out until things improve. If you're dating someone, declare a "timeout" until changes are in the works.

You are experiencing domestic violence

Stomped out. Put down. Demoralized to the point of inaction and lethargy. These can describe the situation of an individual whose mate has done damage to her psyche. People always wonder why women (and sometimes men) stay with partners who abuse them, but those who have lived in such households know all too well that it's a gradual erosion of confidence and a dismantling of self-sufficiency. Soon, the person being hit or demoralized actually comes to believe that he or she is the cause. An abused person may feel too dumb, too poor, or too inept, to make it alone. This person sees no other options.

In truth, there are always alternatives. No matter how incapacitated you feel from daily putdowns, you can find a way out the door to a better life.

You are not happy. If you think you are, review for a minute the panic/anxiety that domestic violence produces. You panic when your mate hits or verbally abuses you. And equally devastating is the daily dread; you're walking on landmines, knowing that any day, one could explode and blast your leg off.

The following are some steps you can take to improve your life:

- Call a hotline for domestic violence.
- Take the steps suggested by a counselor, the first of which will be getting yourself motivated to get out of the house you share with the abuser.
- Follow the legal advice you're provided in the halfway house or the respite home you flee to.
- Make sure that any meeting you have with your mate involves other people nearby; you set up the place, terms, and time limits.
- Remember that a mate who is interested in salvaging the relationship will be able to be "humble" enough to go to any

lengths to reach a workable compromise. And if there is no interest in making changes, you have nothing to work with in the way of this "love," and your only recourse is finding a way to put closure on the relationship.

- Specify clearly what you need from your mate—spell out all of the ways that things must be different in order for you (and your children) to want to live with him again.

You just separated from a mate, or got a divorce

High-level anxiety usually accompanies separation or divorce, even if you're the one instigating it. The depth of disappointment and heartbreak are things that no one can prepare you for—what was once a dream has dissolved or deteriorated into despair or disaster.

You may feel guilt, anger, frustration, insecurity, or depression. You may even go through a period when you desperately want another chance, even though everything points to the obvious—that the relationship is over and that your mate doesn't want to try to save it.

Here are some survival tips:

- Challenge distorted thinking: For example, if you're saying "If I couldn't make it work, I'm so worthless no one's going to want me." Challenge that statement: Are you absolutely sure of that? Of course not.
- Take care of yourself. Use the next few months to get to know yourself, and like yourself, and discover what's important to you the next time you try a relationship.
- Don't be afraid to cry. Talk it over with someone you feel close to—but put limits on how long and how often you'll do this.
- Sort out (and try to understand) your role in the breakdown of the relationship. Are there parts of you that you need to work on? Are there ways you respond to arguments that are nonproductive? Saying you want to improve a few things is not beating up on yourself.
- Make a list of what's good about your life.

- Reduce your anxiety by practicing positive affirmations—praising yourself for the "good parts" of you that undoubtedly will be a delight to those you share yourself with in the future. "People tell me they love my smile. Friends say I'm a fun conversationalist—that's a good thing."

You're experiencing anxiety because you're in a tempestuous relationship

Sometimes, couples get so caught up in being in a bond of sound and fury that they forget that bitter animosity and battles aren't normal for people who love each other. Love should be a positive, mostly happy experience—not one that torments you. Tempestuous relationships bring anxiety...which is bad for your health. So, if that's what you're living with, make some changes.

State your case to your mate and ask for a willingness to make changes. Or ask for some space so you can think things through. In either case, you can use anxiety-busting skills to get you through the initial misery of a breakup. (See Chapter 3.)

- Reassure yourself when doubt sweeps through you. You may get depressed and weepy, but you'll live. After the split, you'll still have someone very important left...and that's you. You will definitely adjust to being without the person you loved.

  While you're still hurting, you may feel like no one in the world has ever experienced the level of horror you're going through—but tell yourself this: "Everyone feels that way." Think how often you've heard a friend share something heartfelt in a way that shows she truly believes hers is an all-new, totally unique brand of heartbreak—something that has never before occurred in human history.

- List things you loved about the relationship, and a second list of things you didn't like. When you get sentimental, get out list number two. That will help you remember that humans have an interesting way of screening out the bad when we get misty-eyed. Put reality therapy to work by rereading that list of funky traits.

- Get to a positive emotional place by seeing friends, going places, and doing things.
- Don't date for a few months, if you can keep from it. Get in touch with yourself again. Love yourself.
- Talk healthy self-talk. "That guy just wasn't right for me, and I wasn't right for him, either. Each of us will be a better match for someone else. The fact that our relationship 'failed' doesn't make either of us bad. Just a pairing that didn't work. I wish him well."
- Wait a few months and then review things that each of you did that were damaging. Listen in your mind to the things you were criticized for, and give them consideration. Discard ones that seem inaccurate. But if your ex made some observations that you've heard before—perhaps, from another person you dated—give those a careful look. Perhaps you are a bit of a nag. That doesn't make you bad; it just makes you someone who needs to work on that trait.
- Take care of things you've been putting off. Make a list.
- Limit admittance to your pity party. When you start feeling sorry for yourself, allow no more than 10 minutes of misery. Then, leave the house to do something kind for someone. Pass your healing time by taking the focus off yourself and putting it on helping others.
- Talk to someone about your sorrow—but keep it short. Don't bend your friend's ear until your pal starts to age before your eyes. Friends like to be confidantes...but with limits. A few sessions of mind-bending, tear-wrenching miseries are plenty. After that, journal daily until you feel like you've cleansed your system of toxic thoughts. Seek emotional closure.

Of course, just as you find you're not thinking about your mate much anymore, you'll probably get a phone call, wanting a do-over. Your mate has changed (translated, that means the relationship he left you for didn't work out).

But statistics tell us that backtracking hardly ever works. The same things that tripped up the relationship the first time will do it the second time. But many people can't resist giving an old lover one more shot. Just remember that when the same lethal issues crop up, you'll have to go through the healing process all over again.

Often, couples give relationships a second or third or 15th try—because they miss the familiar—even if the familiar was severely flawed. But when you hook back up with the old mate out of pity, or because you hate your life, expect to see a replay of disaster. And when the same problems resurface, you'll want to smack yourself for repeating the same mistakes.

Sure, you two had good times—everybody does. But it takes more than a history of a few shared happy evenings for a satisfying relationship. You'd need to see major changes, and rarely do partners want to do that much work.

Finally, if you notice that the old relationship left you with a shaky self-image, seek out positive, upbeat people. Join a group with a focus that interests you—church, book club, sailing club, among others. Cherish friends and relatives.

Every morning when you get out of bed, remind yourself that life is good—and that you're lucky to be alive. Once you're awake and cheered, ask what you can do with your day that you'll enjoy. Don't waste any of your time on earth. Think of the what-if-I-had-six-months-to-live dilemma, and refuse to muck around in the quicksand of remorse.

Break the cycle! People steeped in anxiety tend to pedal through a set of destructive emotions: worry, self-doubt, low moods, social avoidance, and the downward spiral that results, creating a whirlwind of fears.

Step by step, you can regain control and send your negativity packing (see Chapter 4 for the 30-day plan).

Your mate cheated on you

You may be surprised to hear that the majority of couples who experience infidelity actually do stay together afterward...but that doesn't mean the salvaged relationship is a good one. Sometimes, you have a marriage-of-convenience—it's still a guilt-ridden relationship, but the partners decide not to split up for the good of the kids, the finances, or something else that makes sense to them.

This is not a good way to live. For your mental health, you need to work your way to closure on the cheating issue—or you're going to suffer the sky-high anxiety that comes with living with a cheater you still don't trust.

Try these steps:

- Ask your partner when you can have a talk so that both of you can lay your cards on the table. Set up a time and place, free of interruptions and rushing.
- Tell how you have felt since your mate dishonored your trust, and what you would like in order to make living together more comfortable. ("I'd like for you to let me know when you're working late and who's going to be there.")
- Ask for a commitment to help you mend.
- Ask for thoughts on ways to strengthen the bond.
- Thank your mate for telling you his thoughts. If your mate says, "I wanted someone I could talk to, and that's why I had an affair," you'll be tempted to shout back "sounds to me like there wasn't much talking going on," but instead of that, listen. Focus on listening, and on being the person your mate is most comfortable talking to. Give that thought at least 5 minutes of your time.
- Tell your straying mate you want to be able to express your thoughts when you feel distrustful (because of the affair), and ask for patience.

You feel conflicted about staying with your mate

Many times couples stay together out of inertia. Perhaps, the relationship has been deteriorating for years, but both of you were so busy with work and raising children and taking care of parents that you long ago stopped giving energy to your relationship. Now, you look at it and see something in such disrepair that you can't imagine how to get it back on track. Here are some pointers for evaluating what you have:

- List the good parts of the relationship as it is.
- List the things you would like to see changed or improved.

- Think of ways that you could be contributing more to the relationship.
- List ways that your own actions have served to undermine the closeness.
- List needs you have.
- List your mate's needs as you perceive them.

Arrange a time when you and your partner can discuss these things, but first, declare a truce. "Let's try to look at the situation in a calm, dispassionate way, to make things better."

If your mate refuses or thinks the idea is "stupid," then write down your thoughts and give them to him. When you hand over the list, ask when the two of you can meet to discuss some ideas. Tell him that you're very interested in hearing his thoughts.

For anxiety-curbing until you come up with joint solutions, use the skills outlined in Chapter 3.

You're experiencing a great deal of anxiety over your sexual performance

Couples' sex lives are always evolving. No one can "catch and hold onto" that initial blazing chemistry any more than you can put a firefly in a jar and make it live. Work stressors, death, illness, depression—many factors that are natural parts of living can lead to sexual slumps. And sometimes, slumps get worse when one partner gloms on to the symptoms (no interest or dysfunction) as "a sign" or "bad omen."

Typically, a lack of interest in sex, or impotence, is a fleeting thing. Just like a head cold that will pass with time, sexual valleys generally right themselves. Give yourself the right to be disinterested in sex from time to time and still be normal.

At the same time, sex is often enjoyable, and keeping that in mind will get most people back on track. Tips for refueling your own desire are:

- Make overt moves to show your mate what attracted you in the first place; this can be a flower on the desk at the end of the day, a sweet note, a kind gesture or attentiveness to needs.

- Express your feelings openly: "You've probably noticed I've been kind of a sexual slug lately, but the cutbacks at work are really depressing me...."
- Don't be afraid to say what you want from your partner. No matter how long you've been together, it's never too late to improve communication in the bedroom.
- Buy a book about sex or romance or both—and read it for the excitement value. Recall the pleasures of lovemaking in all its glory.
- Learn to talk in bed. Most partners find it helpful when a mate says, "that feels good" or "I like that." The more you get fully engaged—moving, responding, emoting—the easier it is for your mate to get into it.
- If you don't know what pleases your mate the most in bed, ask that question. Be generous with your lovemaking.
- Don't be fearful of doing something new. For example, if your mate always wanted to make love on the patio, get an air mattress and get out there. If no one's around, why not?

You keep obsessing about your second or third marriage ending in divorce

If you have generalized anxiety disorder, obsessing is natural to you. So, worrying about your marriage ending in divorce is something you'll just tack on to your repertoire of worries. While some people get married for the second or third time and just hope for (and expect) the best, you're such a trouble-borrower that you're already listing pitfalls as you exit the aisle.

You may be asking yourself, "What's wrong with me that I always have to question everything?" Well, the truth is, as we've said before, some of us are just worriers. When you were a child being potty trained, you probably fretted when you "delivered" and also when you didn't.

To get a grip on your worry-about-marriage-failure, try these helpful hints:

- Take your fears out to the cliff and jump off—in other words, ask yourself what you will do if the third marriage does fail. Will you die? Will you be sent to prison? Will your relatives refuse to speak to you? Will you lose all your friends? Will you get fired? None of these things will happen, and when you explain that to yourself, it can be reassuring.
- Live for the day at hand. Don't worry about tomorrow; don't think about what you failed to do yesterday. Ask: "What can I do today to make myself happy and help my mate have a better day?"
- Make yourself your mate's best friend. If you can be a dear listener and confidante, if you can make love like there's no tomorrow, if you can make your mate laugh—chances are, you'll never have to worry about a split.
- When you find yourself fretting about divorce and you feel panic-stricken, try self-talk: "Here's what I'll do if that happens—I'll go see my grown daughter, and we'll talk and cry, and then I'll figure out what to do next. I will have a good life, regardless."

You're anxious over your mate's long-term illness/ disability, drug addiction...or discovery of incest

You have to handle the anger, work through the trauma, and figure out how to get rid of the numbness. When you deal with a mate's major problem—from something that he couldn't avoid (illness or disability) to something that could be avoided (incest or drugs)—you'll probably experience gigantic mood swings. At the base of the whole situation, whether the truth has just been revealed, or you're both dealing with the aftermath, you'll feel anxiety-ridden. The coolest person in the world doesn't get through traumas like these unfazed. You may feel irritable, have trouble concentrating, and experience an out-of-body sadness.

Rerunning the horror of what has happened is one of the worst parts. Your mind has that image, and just can't quit showing it, so you see yourself at your mate's deathbed, or you imagine yourself visiting the drug addict in jail, or you remember the day when you discovered the incest.

Here are a few ideas for recovery:

- Give yourself permission to feel bad. Accept that this is not a high time in your life. Having low days, or moody feelings, is natural.
- Do things that occupy your mind and time. Don't spend all your waking hours focusing on your troubles.
- Have a support system. Find someone you can talk to.
- Find your spiritual core. When life makes little sense, many people find amazing solace in church and/or spirituality, re-capturing the feeling that whatever life throws your way, you'll cope and make a good thing of your time on earth.
- Don't deny what happened, or try to rationalize it into insig-nificance. This is a common mistake, particularly in the case of incest. The woman who discovers her mate has had an incestuous relationship is so stunned that she hurries to hide the truth from family, authorities, and especially herself. It is almost as if the failure to face it head on will make it evapo-rate. Unfortunately, no one comes to grips with something traumatic by sweeping it under the rug. Far better to con-front the reality of the event and seek to achieve closure, no matter how long that takes.
- Find your new way of living. After a huge crisis, every single day feels different, and that's because it actually is. You're a different person post-trauma, and you don't feel the same way you did about people who have disappointed you. So, you redefine your sense of "what is" and you go on. Your new reality is the base for your new life script.

8

Getting Rid of Job-Related Anxiety

You just got fired or laid off, and you're worried about finding a job

YOU KNEW IT WAS COMING, OR SUSPECTED IT, BUT NOTHING COULD BE worse than the day you get the news. You've lost your job, and for the past month, during the company buyout and the new takeover, you'd been telling yourself: "I have no idea what I'll do if I get laid off."

Obviously, you could have been planning. Anyone working for a company that's having layoffs should be mapping Plans A, B, and C. But let's presume that you didn't plan. Plus, you just got fired, leaving your body and mind so full of anxiety that your heart is slam-dancing in your chest. Your mind zooms some very scary visions of unpaid bills. You imagine how upset your mate and kids will be.

To reduce your anxiety, change what you're thinking. This will make you feel better than wallowing in self-pity. Allow 30 minutes of feeling sorry for yourself—mind-flowing, brain-numbing self-pity—and then stop it. Any more self-indulgence is a waste of time.

Regroup by doing the following:

- Admit that you're disappointed, but you've been disappointed before and you survived.
- Take this as a sign that you'll make a bold career move—one you might not have been willing to take otherwise. Perhaps, you've wanted to try something totally different. For example, perhaps you want to learn to be an EMT. Get a job that doesn't drain you during the day but does pay the bills.
- Revise your thoughts when your mind dips into the gloomy parts of job-loss. "I'll use the stress I'm feeling to reach new levels of confidence and optimism. My next job will be more 'me' than what I've done in the past."
- Put a positive spin on the situation. When well-meaning relatives and friends ask if you're scared, reframe it: "Yes, but it's also a very exciting time. I've decided to do something I've always wanted to do. Maybe they did me a favor in laying me off."

You're having trouble getting along with coworkers

The anxiety you feel around coworkers can range from minor irritation to full-blown fury. Common stressors are: irritation over coworkers who don't pull their weight, a feeling that people don't give you the help you need to excel at your job, an entitlement that others who aren't as capable are getting ahead just because they have better people skills—the list goes on and on. The question is, how can you defuse the trouble you're having with co-workers before you end up quitting impulsively, or getting fired?

Use these anxiety-curbing skills (described in Chapter 3): anger management, self-talk, and defusing demons.

Your work responsibilities have increased or changed

The conversation in your head can help or hinder the manner in which you deal with disruptions in the workplace. Start by jotting down some of your concerns in list form. Answer yourself: What bothers you most about the changes?

Remember, feeling nervous about the unknown is normal. Situations aren't always stable; sometimes, they are evolving. At the same time, changes in a work environment usually happen for reasons. Think about the "why" behind them—try to see the point of view of the person making them. Avoid the tendency to judge. Look at management decisions like a person who just walked in off the street.

If you've heard rumors about layoffs, demotions, new bosses "from the outside," accept that you feel shaky. Contemplating change does that. Set out to acquire skills to deal with changes without having panic attacks, and perhaps, without jeopardizing your job.

Here's an approach that may work for you. Look at the reality, and turn it over in your mind. For example: "I have a new boss because of the merger, and the projects we've been working on for a year are being bumped to the back burner, never to be used again. I feel frustrated and scared that I'll lose my job because now there's not much for my department to do."

Okay, now that you've confronted your beast, stop complaining and look at your options. Figure out how you're going to respond to the revised office script. Never assume that you have no choices and that you're locked in forever to an uncomfortable situation. That's just not the case, ever.

Here are some self-talk responses you can use:

- "I can give my new boss a chance, and try not to have preconceived notions or be influenced by what I've heard about her."
- "I can choose not to cope with the discomfort of staying here, and start looking for a new job and a fresh start."
- "I can try doing something entirely new—a job that I've always found intriguing but never had the guts to leave my current comfort level and try."

- "I can brighten my attitude by making a choice that's my own and not the company's. I can decide to stay and be optimistic, look for a job and let the prospect of a new start brighten my spirits, quit, and use my savings to tide me over while I do my job search."
- "I'll remind myself that I am creating my own reality. In other words, if I continually tell myself that the job I'm in looks grim and I'm going to be miserable, I'll make that come true—even though it won't be a conscious thing. If I swear to myself 'I'd go nuts if I stayed around here with this crazy new boss,' then I'll make that a reality. So, I'll write a new script: 'I can make this year better than last year because I'll mold it to fit my needs.' Another possibility: 'I'll get through this changeover because I have strong coping skills. When I feel anxiety, I'll remember that I have options. A change at work doesn't suddenly make me a victim.' Another line of self-talk: 'I have irons in the fire that give me several ways to turn the situation in a productive direction.' If necessary, I'll carry a list of positive self-talk with me and glance at it when I feel anxious."

And what happens if one of your routes goes sour? Then brainstorm with a friend outside the workplace or with yourself. "Okay, that was a dead-end, so I think I'll try this."

Decrease anxiety by imagining what you'll do if a certain thing happens. "My anxiety is creeping up, so I need to control the way my imagination goes. I can take it in a positive direction."

You hate your job

No wonder you're feeling anxious! We spend so much of our lives at our jobs that finding satisfaction in our work is pivotal.

Typically, this one doesn't get better, and you'll probably become such a whiner that friends and family will want to run when they hear you start talking about your work. So, figure out an escape route.

The job isn't you. It's not working for you. So, have the courage to get out. Here are some guidelines:

- Scale up your expectations and seek a situation that's more interesting to you.

- Don't stay in a job that doesn't give you a sense of fulfillment.
- Remember that job changes come in several versions: You can take on new responsibilities in your current job that will pave your way into another position or department; you can do the same kind of work for another company that has more room for advancement; or you can change your profession altogether.
- Realize that just planning for a job change will lift your spirit. Instead of sitting around and moping, you're turning your malaise into a kick in the butt.

You have fears concerning public speaking

"That's just who I am—I can't talk in front of groups."

You can probably relate to that statement. But saying, "that's just who I am," doesn't solve the problem—especially if learning how to speak in public would advance your career.

Remember those attempts to struggle to your feet and give a speech? Many of us have felt that overwhelming sense of impending disaster. And if it's not a full-blown panic attack, it's certainly as scary as one.

Review your situation. Maybe you have awful fears about public speaking but you don't really have to do it to succeed—not in your work or your personal life. Do you need this skill? Do you really want to try to master it? If you don't, then take it off your worry plate. You've probably got something else on there that's more in need of immediate attention.

On the other hand, if you do need to overcome your fear of public speaking, focus on doing that. You can make a small change that will have a big impact on what you're able to accomplish in your life.

Instead of reacting to the spiral of panic coming from public speaking, sit with your feelings and let them simmer. Make a decision to behave your way out of the crucible of fear that's attached to speaking before a group. Take on an approach filled with bravado, and expect yourself to succeed.

When you feel fear making your lips quiver, tell yourself to switch the focus to concentrating on the people you're looking at;

make eye contact with them, smile at them, and get ready to talk to them. And, what if your voice does shake? Or your mouth trembles?

Tell yourself: "No one will die over it, and I'll probably calm down after a few minutes." If you want to spiff up before you do a speaking engagement, join a breakfast club for professionals, and you'll get chances to overcome your speaking fear.

Here are some guidelines that will help you prepare for a less stressful moment at the podium:

1. Make sure you have prepared yourself well in advance. Know what you're going to say, and do the whole thing in front of a mirror to make sure you're inserting enough smiles.
2. Avoid the jitters by not consuming too much caffeine. Eat a good breakfast, lunch, or dinner at the mealtime preceding your speaking engagement.
3. Have small cards with notes on them to cue you to key points, but keep the ideas flowing from your heart and mind. A reader isn't going to catch an audience's attention.
4. Set a glass of water nearby in case your mouth does dry up.
5. Speak slowly and deliberately, and don't worry about the audience's rating you. Most of them have felt what you're feeling—so go forward with confidence. You have something to share with people—and that's a good thing.

You feel anxiety over employees' dislike of you or your hard-hitting managerial approach

The fact that you have passion to do a good job is commendable. But what if your take-no-prisoners attitude makes employees flinch when you walk down the hall? That is not a good thing.

A boss who is always wreaking havoc is most loathsome. This isn't because he or she lacks endearing qualities—but because, mainly, there is a lack of empathy for the employees, along with self-absorption.

A big-picture approach is better, and most companies will be quick to tell supervisors that the boss who tries to help employees succeed will do better as well.

To reduce the anxiety that comes from your very own "bully complex," try the following:

- Before you jump to criticize an employee, stop and gather your thoughts. Is this the best way to get good results, or will you just make someone mad, and thus, less inclined to want to deliver what you ask for?
- Soften up your exchanges. Tell coworkers what you would like to see happen—the end result—and avoid using the emotion-packed words "never" and "always" (as in, "you never do what I ask you to," or "I've never seen you get a report in on time").
- Find a way to make a strong statement in a way that doesn't turn people off.
- Don't seek to intimidate; instead, seek to see a job completed through cooperation between supervisor and staff.

You're experiencing job-review or job-interview anxiety

Many people have extreme cases of jitters related to job evaluations and job interviews. However, you can fix it so that you're the one most likely to get a good review and the last employee who would be laid off if cutbacks came.

Here are tips for getting yourself so entrenched you won't have to worry about losing your job, much less getting a poor review:

- Come up with new ideas to submit to your supervisor; show that you're always "on," striving to do a more innovative job.
- Knock yourself out—have an amazing work ethic. Supervisors love hardworking employees. When others are flying out the door at 5 o'clock every day, make a point of putting in extra time that shows how dedicated you are to finishing your work and delivering strong "product."
- Never make the mistake of "laying low." If your department barely knows you're there, firing you when times get tough won't make a ripple in productivity or morale.
- Put yourself out there. Show that you initiate work projects; volunteer to help others who are running out of time on a project and need assistance.

- Make sure you're known as a big producer.
- Do quality work that is above reproach: neat, mistake-free, and smart.
- Don't be a whiner. Every office has folks who spend too many hours a week bitching and complaining about work overload or others' failure to do what they should—the list could go on and on. It doesn't have to.
- Keep your focus on continuing to develop in your profession.
- Look at chaotic work situations as opportunities to shine: Come up with better, more-efficient ways your squad can turn out the work.
- Keep your skill-set sharp.
- Keep your personal life private.

Your mean boss causes you constant anxiety

When you hear your boss—the spawn of Satan—coming down the hall, you may literally quake in your boots. But that won't help you cope any better. So, what's the best way to defuse your anxiety?

Look at reality. Having a boss who demeans you is no picnic and it's good to acknowledge that. You feel angry and upset, and those are natural reactions to a nasty situation. But don't share your sorrow with coworkers. Take your complaints home to a mate, a friend, or a parent. Talk through your fears with someone you're sure you can trust.

Also, use the "What's the worst thing that can happen?" exercise. Play your gnarly situation out to the bitter end in your mind. No, you won't die from having a mean boss, have a heart attack, go insane, or lose your job. So, what you're looking at is coming up with a self-saving way to cope when you must interact with this devil-tailed individual.

Let's say the demon walks into your office and yells about a report. "This is pathetic! You'd never be able to keep a job in New York where I last ran an office. They'd fire you in two seconds."

Take a deep breath, and decide whether there is any information you could learn from. Tell your boss, "I hear what you're saying, and I'll try to improve my work." You have nothing to gain from sparring.

But do give yourself permission to dislike the way this supervisor treats you and others. And don't cower. Remember, you survived before your boss got there, and you'll survive after this nasty person is gone.

If you come in contact with this supervisor often and you feel anxiety-ridden much of the time, start job-hunting. Be a survivor. You know where the door is.

You obsess about workplace violence

We've all seen it on TV—the employee with an ax to grind returns to his place of employment and shoots people. It's a grim reminder of the unpredictable world we live in today—and a good reason to fortify yourself with coping skills that will help you live a satisfying life without constantly looking over your shoulder.

Thought-stopping is an effective way to deal with this problem. When you feel the fear escalating, stop in mid-fret. Yes, you do have ample reason for concerns—but worrying won't change things one bit. Turn attention to being productive and you'll see how quickly a "refocus" of energy can zap your fears.

You experienced a traumatic workplace betrayal

Getting stabbed in the back by a coworker can give you many sleepless nights. You may be writing "mental letters" to the villain, or thinking how you'll "show" that person he was wrong. But the more energy you devote to vengeance, the more wrought up with anxiety you become.

It's fine to share your shock and disappointment over a workplace betrayal with your mate or a close friend, but leave it alone after that. Don't tell every person at work how mad you are; they can't do anything to help, and worse, they'll probably feed off the excitement of your fury.

Do things that will relax you. If you haven't worked out lately, take out some of your frustration out on weight machines or free weights. Go see a mindless movie with a friend. Take a child on a picnic.

Don't drown your sorrows in alcohol, drugs, food, or cigarettes. Do admit that you're miserable and disappointed—and that you have every right to feel that way. Someone you thought was your friend betrayed you, and that feels awful. But you weren't the only person ever singled out for this perverse form of torture—and you won't be the last.

Keep things in perspective. Your job isn't your life; family and friends should rate higher on your scale. And if that's not the case, you have bigger problems than workplace betrayal!

Give yourself a week to be furious and then say "enough." Move on. The more you backtrack and give power to the hurtful incident, the more anxiety you create inside. Plus, you've allowed the "former friend" to injure you time after time.

You're experiencing job boredom or overload

At home, you can talk to your mate or a parent about this problem. But don't grouse about boredom or overload at work.

When you feel the anxiety welling up inside, turn to something that will lower your pressured feeling. Listen to music. Call a friend who's calming (and not hyper). Chat with a family member who'll be delighted to hear your voice when you call.

Plan activities after work and on weekends so you have things to look forward to. If you're so bummed out that you want to switch jobs entirely, look into that possibility. Sometimes, just the act of looking around can be liberating. Telling yourself, "this isn't the only job in the world that I can do" frees you up to decide if you can tolerate the boredom or overload, or if you'd prefer to find another job (more exciting or less demanding).

You worry about your lack of computer savvy

Feeling behind the curve in a high-tech world gives many people anxiety today. So, get ready to challenge distorted thinking. If you tell yourself you're going to get fired and replaced with a computer wizard, examine the truthfulness of that statement: Is this likely, or are you overreacting simply because you're frightened? Zero in on your real situation and consider the following options:

• Stay right where you are and learn nothing new. This may well limit your acceleration in the workplace—is that a concern?

- Take a course to improve your computer skills. It might be worth the time and money because of the payoffs—increased confidence and job security.
- Don't demonize the computer. You can use it to increase your productivity.
- Accept that your learning curve may be slow and difficult...and that this is quite all right.

You obsess about your inability to get large amounts of work done

Are you too hard on yourself, and your perceived "failings" fill you with anxiety? Or do others you work with act as if you're holding things up with your slowness?

If the first is the case, you're just a perfectionist. You need to remember that your job is part of your life and not your *entire* life. Do be efficient with your workload, but pull out a thought-stop when you move into that place where you're beating yourself up for not doing more. Nothing good can come of a vicious circle of self-recriminations, so stop it!

If your coworkers tell you to produce more, try to deliver what they need if it's realistic. Do you need to focus more fully? If you simply can't meet the demands of the job, look for work that doesn't have built-in frustrations—one that you can handle with the skills and brain that you have.

You're a stressed-out high-achiever

Garden-variety perfectionists should not be confused with those people who are obsessed with perfection to the point that they have the life-ruining obsession called obsessive-compulsive disorder (OCD). Although the first experiences constant frustration because she has standards that few can reach, the latter is ruled by persistent thoughts and impulses. Accompanied by anxiety, obsessional thoughts can be morbid, repulsive, or tedious. OCD sufferers typically develop rituals (hand-washing, triple-checking, among other behaviors) and often hide the secret rather than looking for treatment.

Sometimes anxiety spins out of control and manifests itself in obsessive-compulsive behaviors. In the case of one doctor, the odd habit of hoarding emerged. This man (Paul*) did not want to "let go" of anything that had come to him and was, by all rights, his. (Note, however, that hoarding behavior in human beings can range from normal collecting to pathological self-neglect.)

Paul felt anxious because he didn't think that his family and other people were sufficiently awed by the things he had accomplished. This "lack of appreciation" made him hold on to every piece of mail that saluted his "importance." Although one of the best-known professionals in his field, he felt like no one cared. He stored stacks and stacks of old letters, papers—even wrappers off gifts people had given him. Paul hated having people around him who were less goal-oriented, which included everybody he knew. He kept three beepers clipped to his clothes at all times; he carried two cell phones; he worked 10 to 12 hours a day.

His doctor prescribed an SSRI and began behavior therapy. He gradually weaned Paul off of his "treasures," starting small and working up. Paul coped well with the anxiety of having a few things removed, and then moved on to having a larger number of items taken away. Finally, he faced an office with only minimal reminders of his "greatness."

Throughout, he journaled why it would not work and why he needed his things. His doctor gently dissected each objection.

Paul learned breathing techniques, and imagined himself less stressed and more happy. He went from six cups of coffee a day to one; diet improvements included cuts in sugar intake, protein enhancement, and increased hydration.

Treating OCD with behavior therapy can work well and often has lasting benefits. Effective measures are identifying triggers of obsessions, rituals, and discomfort; designing exposure-and-ritual-prevention goals; and monitoring exposure-and-ritual-prevention sessions until they become habits.

9

Taking Charge of Extended-Family Situations

Anxiety-Busting Tools for This Chapter:
- Changing responses to cues.
- Thought-stopping.
- Anger management.
- Relationship-building.
- Bolstering with nurturing and compassion.

A parent has just come to live in your home

AS A BABY BOOMER, YOU KNOW YOU'RE BLESSED TO HAVE YOUR PARENT still living. But at the same time, you lead a busy life, and the extra responsibility can cause anxiety. Here are some ways to cope:

- Acknowledge that you're worried about how this will work out, and accept that you feel conflicted.
- Think of ways to decompress when you feel overwhelmed by the responsibilities of parenting, taking care of your own parent, holding down a full-time job, and housekeeping and cooking.
- Tell your parent what he could do to be helpful—this is a good thing for both of you. Everyone loves to feel useful.

- Vow that you won't wallow in guilt. It's easy to feel like you're not doing enough, that you're not patient enough, and on and on.
- Accept that you won't be able to create an "ideal" situation.
- Arrange for caregiving help if your father's health is deteriorating and caring for him is time-consuming.
- Don't get mad at yourself for feeling frustrated when your relative's mind fades and it seems like you're dealing with a stranger.
- Take him places. Even a trip to the grocery store is refreshing to someone who can't drive anymore and is stuck surrounded by four walls.
- Encourage telling stories about his childhood, your childhood, family, etc. Laugh together, smile, tease.
- Make time to sit quietly, hold hands, and express your love. Bring him a surprise—a book, a flower. Do happy things for him while you still have him, and you'll always be glad you did.

An interfering in-law disturbs you, or you wonder how you're faring with your mate's family

You get two feet inside your relative's front door for a Christmas visit, and you can already feel the gritty bite of being sized up. That kind of in-law moment can make you anxious very quickly, but you can call on your new skills to defuse your anxiety.

In most families, you'll find people you click with, and ones with whom there's a huge disconnect. Also, some people are born criticizers; you may be facing one who just doesn't mind making you feel uncomfortable.

What's most likely, however, is that you're exaggerating the situation. You have a feeling someone doesn't like you as much as the Last Wife That Donny Joe Had, and you could be right. But chances are, your in-laws don't hate you, either. Remember, they're more interested in what you think of them—that's pretty much always the case with people. So, kill them with kindness. "But they'll still find something to criticize about me!" you say. Probably, but they'll have less to work with. And maybe they'll sound petty, even to themselves.

De-stress when you're around them by changing your responses to their cues. A putdown doesn't require a comeback. You can decide not to let them get to you, and then behave so that it happens.

Your parent or sibling is getting a divorce

Be there. Let your loved one talk it through. If she feels like crying, you've got a comforting shoulder. Try some of the following to decrease your own anxiety that comes from vicariously experiencing your relative's stress.

- Get over the idea that you can control the split-up or fix it. And help your relative to be realistic about "what is."
- Encourage her to understand that the two of them just weren't good together—that means no judgment on either party.
- Let her talk about what went wrong and don't try to set the record straight.
- Watch for signs of depression or anxiety, and be there to take her to dinner, or to rent a movie and make some popcorn.
- Provide support-talk. When your sister says, "Albert dumped me—he doesn't love me anymore," your comeback is: "but lots of people do love you, and someday, another man will, too. You're a special woman, and people do love you." Make her laugh: "You know, maybe the guy really isn't tear-worthy."

An ex-spouse is giving you and your kids grief

Your ex-spouse rails at you when the children come to visit on weekends—and he rails when they don't. He doesn't like their hairstyles, clothes, actions, and he likes yours even less. No one needs this kind of grief.

But when your ex has visitation rights, you're stuck in a crucible with him for 10 or 15 years, so try the following ways of coping:

- Give him the benefit of the doubt—being a part-time parent is tough. Have some heart for that predicament.
- Try not to speak ill of an ex. Instead, let your children know the nice things about their father—why you fell in love with him in the first place. Don't harp on his faults.
- Express your appreciation when he pays child support, shows up for a soccer game, etc.
- Ask him to call you on the phone to settle problems.
- Remember all those nice things you learned in church and use them. An ex is a fellow human being, and he's someone's child. Find kindness in your heart for him—that's a great gift for your children.

A family member's mental illness makes you anxious

Your sister-in-law has been diagnosed as schizophrenic, and you're worried: Will your children have that gene? Will your husband show signs of it someday? Will it be safe to leave your kids in her care?

First, find out everything you can about the disorder. Refuse your anxiety by discovering what you should be doing to deal effectively and compassionately with this relative—and do those things. If you have trouble with empathy, rent or buy the film *A Beautiful Mind,* and take a lesson from the wife's heart-based way of dealing with schizophrenia.

10

Knocking the Panic Out of Personal Issues

Anxiety-Busting Tools for This Chapter:

- Avoiding blame-shifting.
- Anger management.
- Changing responses to cues.
- Defusing demons by sorting beliefs.
- Role-playing.
- Assertiveness training.
- Effective expression of needs.

You have extreme anxiety about aging

MIDLIFE CRISIS MAY HAVE SEEMED LIKE A FOREIGN CONCEPT WHEN you first heard about it, back when you were a college kid. But as you've moved into your 40s, it's as scary as having a tarantula in your bedroom. You never really planned to have this crisis in your life.

Mary Beth* began obsessing about getting older the year she turned 40, but she didn't have real "aging issues" until she was 49. With her 50th birthday a near and present danger, she became a nutcase. She wondered why she had accomplished so little by this point; she was having problems with her grown kids; she hated looking old. She even began having panic attacks when she went to trendy restaurants.

Finally, she turned to a doctor and explained what disturbed her: When Mary Beth looked in the mirror, she hated seeing wrinkles and gray hair, and had begun lying about her age. In addition, her 20-year-old daughter hated her job, which made Mary Beth feel guilty—she should have steered her toward a better career. Her son was addicted to cocaine.

First, her counselor offered her a good mantra for midlife: "We've all been 25 and we got to enjoy that. And the woman who's 25 will someday be 50, if she's lucky." There are seasons in life; this doesn't have to feel disastrous—just different. Each age has advantages. Her counselor cited Mary Beth's assets: She was a respected lawyer who was well set financially, she traveled a great deal, she had friends, and she was close to her grown kids.

Mary Beth tried to focus on the positive parts of growing older. Her counselor suggested using her strengths to help others. She volunteered at a women's center that helped young women in distress (domestic abuse victims). She found the work very rewarding.

Mary Beth bought some clothes and had a makeover. She got new makeup styling, instruction on application, a manicure, a pedicure, and went to a new hairstylist who was a little edgier. With updated makeup and highlights in her drab blonde hair, she felt prettier. She had an eyelid lift because the bags under her eyes made her look tired; people were always saying she looked exhausted.

Each day she worked on framing aging more positively. She extended that period of excellent thoughts. Now, could she get rid of her panic attacks?

When she felt panic rising, she examined her chain of negative thoughts: "What if I go to lunch and people look at me like I'm invisible? I'm not a looker anymore, and that scares me. I'll have a panic attack, I just know it!"

She talked herself down from the ledge this way: "Lunch with a friend will still be fun. My friend is glad to be with me. If other diners think I'm old, it doesn't matter. Being ignored is not catastrophic. Some people are ignored lifelong, and still have good lives."

Now, when she worries about having a panic attack, Mary Beth confronts her fear and breaks it into small, manageable parts. Through role-playing, she walks herself through a worst-case scenario in which two young men snicker as she walks by—and one of them says, "What's that old bag doing wearing such a short skirt?"

She thinks, "What do they know about me? I'm a good and fun person. It doesn't matter that neither would ask me out. Maybe I would pass on them, too. Younger does not necessarily mean better."

Mary Beth realized that she punished herself when she thought about her children because that was more acceptable to her than being upset with her kids. She decided to shed her over-responsibility complex. She explained to them: "I can't make your lives good—you have to do that by making good choices." She offered to get her son into a rehab program, which he accepted. Her daughter asked her advice on pursuing a different career.

Mary Beth experienced no more panic attacks after a month of reconditioning. She learned to enjoy the youth in others. She would see a woman in the bloom of youth and admire her beauty; she'd see an 80-year-old woman and admire the character in her lined face. Finally comfortable in her 50-year-old skin, she began working out at a gym. Her kids admired her changes and accepted her letting them handle their own problems.

She no longer bought into the idea that midlife was a crisis; it felt full of promise. A friend called and asked if she was "emotionally available." Mary Beth went on a blind date with a man nine years her junior. Having come to grips with her aging issues, she was able to have a good time and focus on her date. Three years later, Mary Beth is enjoying a terrific second phase of her life. There is, indeed, life after 50.

You worry about your shyness and inadequacies

Panic hits when you have to face a situation in which you feel like people will be looking at you and evaluating how you're performing socially.

To quell the anxiety welling up inside, try the following:

- Rewrite what shyness means. Tell yourself it's actually okay that you're not the noisiest or most talkative person in the room. That doesn't make you a bore or an airhead.

- Remember that most people feel inadequate in some way. Knowing that each person in the room has feelings of inadequacy will help you to relax and think "hey, it's okay that I'm not sure my outfit is 'casual chic' enough for this casual chic event. I showed up—that counts."
- Accept and give compliments. If someone compliments your outfit, thank that person instead of saying "what—this old thing?" When you see something you admire, say so ("You have great hair"). However, in the workplace, don't overdo this to the point that someone could mistake your praise as a come-on.
- Listen well when you interact with others. If an issue comes up and you don't agree, just acknowledge what the other person has said ("I can see that you feel strongly about this") but don't feel like you must set the record straight, or abandon your own beliefs.
- State what you want matter-of-factly: "I'd like for you to give me a call and fill me in on the details."
- Prepare yourself for occasions when you'll be interacting with someone who has upset you in the past. Have a comment ready to go: "It bothers me when you tell me you'll do something with me and then you bail at the last minute."
- Gear up to respond to people who minimize you: "I want you to know that I'd like to cook dinner for our club sometime, but it hurts my feelings when you keep reminding me that I'm overdue. I know that already."
- Abandon the feeling that you have no say in things. How you feel matters. But you have to make people aware that you're a living, breathing, engaged individual.

Beginning menopause is making you anxious

You're not a kid anymore—that's abundantly clear. Turn that fact over and over and revel in the pluses: You're established in your career and actually feel like you know what you're doing. Your kids have finished college or are situated in jobs. Friends and family know what you're all about and accept you.

You don't have to view The Change as creepy, mysterious, or ominous. Some women breeze right through menopause without a blip on the radar screen; those are the ones you never see on talk shows.

To address your anxiety, try the following:

- Accept what's going on and decide what you're going to do. Do you want to take estrogen replacement therapy to get rid of the insomnia and hot flashes? Or do you prefer a more natural approach, such as using herbal supplements?
- Get off the "What have I accomplished?" merry-go-round. Most people at midlife have done some of the things they wanted to do, and missed out on others. You're not a loser just because you haven't made your first million, snagged a great guy, or reached your spiritual pinnacle.

You're dealing with an unplanned pregnancy or rape

The anxiety of an unplanned pregnancy or rape can be extreme. You need a confidante, be it a friend, relative, anonymous-hotline voice, or counselor. Be proactive in reporting the rape. Ask for a rape counselor to be at your side as you go through the steps involved in the medical exam, reports, and so forth.

To deal with an unplanned pregnancy, talk with the person you're closest to—and if you aren't close to anyone, go to a minister or a women's center and meet with a counselor. For some women, an unplanned pregnancy presents one of life's biggest crossroads and most difficult decisions, so your being armed with good information and spiritual guidance can go a long way toward helping you make a decision you can live with.

Neither situation is one that you will get through without anxiety, but having someone's help and support will ease the distress.

Four million American women suffer from post-traumatic stress disorder resulting from aggravated assault, rape, or non-crime-related trauma. Behavior-modification techniques can help soothe your anxiety. Two effective treatments are: providing prolonged exposure to the stressor, and teaching the patient how to inoculate herself against the stressor. During prolonged exposure, the woman revisits her traumatic memory and recounts it in detail. The description is audiotaped, and she listens to it, as homework. A growing familiarity with the events dilutes the power of the fear.

To inoculate against stress, you can try controlled breathing, thought-stopping, preparation for stressors, and role-playing. These types of treatments are effective when used to soothe chronic post-traumatic stress disorder in women after traumatic sexual or non-sexual assault.

You feel stressed about planning a wedding or another big event

Big-event anxiety can cause upheavals in people who aren't normally inclined to get stressed. Try the following to handle your stress:

- Specify a goal for the event, which should be something like this: "I want to have an event that's fun for the people who attend...and for me."
- List what it would take to meet that goal: Make sure all elements of the wedding are taken care of well in advance. Find things that people have enjoyed at weddings you've attended in the past. Decide what would make you happy in the way of a "successful" event. For example, "My daughter and her new husband would love the wedding, I'd dance a lot, and there would be lots of people there."
- Make a list of things you can do (that are under your control) in order to make those things happen. Also, list things that you can't control: "I can't control how many people come, or if my friends will attend—and that's okay."
- List your worries about the event and challenge each one. "What if people don't like the place we chose for the reception?" Challenge that one and you'll know that you'll be surrounded by caring friends and family—not the "event police." If judgmental folks are among those invited, maybe you'll be lucky and they won't come. Another worry: "What if people don't come because the weather's bad?" Put this on your list of things you can't control. Generally speaking, most people

who plan to go to an event don't back out just because of foul weather. They have already set aside the evening, so the tendency is to go through with their plan. If attendance is down about 10 percent because it rains, you can deal with that.

- Stick with a balanced diet and exercise program. This will help you deal more effectively with stressors.
- Ask for help. Family members and friends have said "let me know what I can do," so take them up on their offers. Delegate small tasks.
- Don't beat yourself up with "shoulds": "If I were a good parent, I'd have more money, and this would be a better wedding." Hit the delete button on that one. You have what you have. And no amount of panic will change that. Focus on being a joyful person who contributes, concentrating on friends and family. Smile. Laugh. Enjoy being with your guests. Shower your grownup kid with love—that's what lingers in memories.
- And during event-planning, don't make major issues of push-pull situations. Be your calmest, least-confrontational self.

You worry that you're a bore

Are you abnormally afraid of meeting new people and socializing with them? Do you fear criticism? Do you feel funny when you have to eat around other people?

Most social phobics avoid what makes them feel anxious. But, this only underscores the truth—that the only coping mechanism they have is avoiding things, which increases their anxiety.

Consider the following ways of decreasing your anxiety levels:

- When you are in a social setting, watch how your anxiety goes down as the evening progresses (you don't stay at a high level the entire time).
- Condition yourself to go places. You have to stop your pattern of avoiding social situations, or you'll become more disabled as your phobia controls more of your life. Must-show events may become too much for you to face.

- Accept that "showing up" may feel fairly uncomfortable at first. Maybe it'll be uncomfortable the second time. But you'll become "desensitized" by repeated exposures.
- Distract yourself by deciding before leaving home what you'll do if you feel panicky—take your mind to your Sun Scene.
- Consider your worst expectations: "People will hope they don't get stuck talking to me. People will think I'm dressed wrong. People will yawn if they have to talk to me. I'll have nothing to say." Then, make yourself address each fear separately. Does it matter if someone hates what you're wearing? So what if someone yawns? If you run out of things to talk about, rest assured that happens to the most gregarious people in the world occasionally. You will live to go home again.
- Defuse your fear. If momentarily focusing on a picture on the wall helps, try that. If thinking of the acceptance your child gives you makes you feel good, savor that thought. Wrap yourself up in the coziest zone of loving people you know, and think how much they cherish you.

You're traumatized from the death of a mate, child, parent, or a catastrophic global event

This is one of the most difficult stressors. You'll go through shock and grieving and denial and anger, only to experience these over and over again. Losing someone you love leaves a void that is never filled. The only thing that changes is realigning your thoughts so that you can reach some level of acceptance that allows you to go forward.

Allow yourself a few days of weeping and wailing—but not months of it. Resist attempts on the part of your logic to try to make sense of the death. You'll feel numb from the absolute nonsensical nature of loss.

Do, however, try to cherish what you have left: warmth, loyalty, love, and memories. These aren't diminished by time. Work to reestablish a spiritual partnership with the person who died, so you can share experiences: "If my mother were here at my daughter's wedding, she would be loving every minute of it. No one would love it more." You will learn to think such thoughts with the wonderment of how special that person was, not with a feeling of tortured loss.

Your best bet for lifting yourself up is to help someone else in the family who is grieving the same loss.

You're battling drug or alcohol addiction

Get help. Find a treatment program, or ask your physician for a recommendation. Today, many who administer programs for overcoming drug and alcohol addiction offer an individualized approach called "treatment matching," which is an excellent way to deal with drug and alcohol problems. This is one of the newest form of rehab, tailored to the particular individual. Detox, treatment, and aftercare are designed to suit what looks promising for that person's preferences, temperament, and special problems.

Back home, you'll follow an aftercare regimen, and devise your own tricks for handling anxiety. Previously, you turned to alcohol or drugs when you were under pressure, so consider some of the following replacements:

- Ask someone to serve as your lifeline if you feel yourself slipping.
- Change things. If you can't be with old friends without resorting to drugging or drinking, stay away from them for however long it takes to get a handle on your addiction. If you must be around people who drink or use illegal drugs, be prepared to refuse their offers to share.
- Nurture yourself with exercise and good nutrition. Change your old slacker ways that went with the drugs and alcohol.
- Find substitutes for old standbys. Indulge in hard candy, pretzels, or barbecue potato chips. Find something you can turn to when you want to go back to your destructive indulgence.
- Surround yourself with positive people. If you don't know any, go to a church, synagogue, or some kind of spiritual program and you'll find some.
- Stay as busy as possible.
- Try to reestablish old connections with family and friends.
- Expect withdrawal symptoms to be tough and ask your doctor or counselor how to handle these.

- Expect staying sober and drug-free to be difficult. Remember that you want a different life, and you can get there, even if you suffer setbacks.

You want to stop smoking but anxiety overwhelms you

You get swift reassurance from lighting up a cigarette because of nerve-soothing nicotine. So, the additive drug that's causing damage to your lungs, heart, and circulatory system is also binding you to it, and that's why managing to quit smoking can be one of the hardest challenges a person can undertake. However, people do it every day. And most of those who succeed have tried a few times and failed. If you already have a few failed attempts under your belt, you're closer to the finish line.

You can try a formal smoking cessation program (these are offered by community centers, hospitals, and clinics) or you can do it on your own. First, you have to make the decision and firm it up. Then, cut down to a specific number of cigarettes a day. Decide, for example, that you will only have a cigarette when you wake up, one after lunch, one after dinner, and one before bed. In a couple of weeks, cut this down, and keep going until you give up the last one. Also, get rid of all cigarettes except the number you're allowing yourself.

- Check with your doctor about smoking-cessation aids. He may recommend that you use a nicotine patch, spray, or gum; a nicotine inhaler; or a prescription medication (Zyban) that reduces anxiety and helps prevent weight gain.
- Set up new patterns. If you have always had a cigarette when you woke up in the morning, now you're going to munch on licorice or drink a glass of coke or tea.
- Don't believe that voice in your mind that's saying "you need a cigarette right now." The truth is, you want one, but you don't need one. Rerun your mental image of how you will look and act once you can walk a flight of stairs without huffing and puffing. You can live without wanting to race out for a cigarette.

- Get your car spiffed up with new-car fragrance, and remind yourself of the putrid smell people complained of when they rode in your car.
- Have your clothes cleaned, but keep one tobacco-smelling shirt just for a reminder of the funky odor.
- Surround yourself with symbols of how society is now anti-smoking: ads for apartments that lease only to nonsmokers, job listings for nonsmokers only, and so forth.
- Reward yourself with dinner at a great restaurant for each week you stay tobacco-free.
- Ask friends to inquire about whether you're still not smoking so that you'll have to confess or brag.
- Try an online stop-smoking program, such as *QuitNet.com*.

You have a life-threatening illness

If this is new to you, you're probably still going through grieving the change in your life—fear, anger, denial, and so forth. Acceptance of your illness may be slow to come, if it does at all. But if you've been living with a life-threatening illness for a long time, you've probably found a way to face your situation...but that doesn't mean you've loosened the grip of panic or anxiety.

Here are some ideas for dealing effectively with a life-threatening illness and its problems, such as chemotherapy:

- Locate support groups and people who can lend help and can listen when you need to air your thoughts.
- Acknowledge how you feel. For example, if you're a parent, you may be experiencing guilt because you know that you're doing to die soon, and this feels like letting your children down. Much of your life has been devoted to filling the needs of your children and protecting them, so you naturally will have the desire to "control" this situation, which, of course, you can't do.
- Seek ways of finding peace: church, yoga, spiritual readings, and so forth. Study philosophies on what happens after death, and find reassurance in knowing what you think about that.

You're experiencing sexual dysfunction

See a therapist or physician to discuss your concerns. Often, dysfunction stems from a physical problem that can be "fixed" with medication or counseling. If you don't want to talk to anyone, you can try the following ways of dealing with the matter on your own:

- Accept that sexuality is not a static thing. Your interest has peaks and valleys. Your performance may vary with the state of your health, your partner, or separation or divorce.
- Review what gives you pleasure and see if there's anything else you would like to do with your partner that you have never done in the past. If so, try to establish open communication on what is fulfilling to you and ask what pleases your mate.
- Set aside time for sex. Lives lived in the fast lane often result in putting sex on hold when most of your focus goes to children, business, or life in general.

Your failing hearing and vision make you feel anxious

Instead of being in denial about your failing hearing or vision, seek help. You may need glasses, contacts, a hearing aid, medication, or an operation. Find a way to get the most out of the sense that is failing.

Then, don't panic about your diminished sense. Let those in your inner circle know what's happening: "I can't hear very well anymore, and my hearing aid only does a little bit of good, so please speak up." If people act as if hearing loss equals dementia, set the record straight with good humor: "You don't need to worry about my mind having failed along with my hearing; I'm the same old me—I just can't hear very well."

Don't continue to drive when you know you can't see well enough. Ask for help from friends and/or family. You can't put lives in jeopardy just because it's hard to admit you can't see well enough to drive and you hate losing your independence.

You obsess about inheriting the gene for cancer

Some types of cancer are familial in nature. If you know that you may have that genetic potential, you may experience a great deal of anxiety.

To deal with it, you can be tested to discover if indeed your genetics carry the cancer gene. Or you may not want to—some folks are horrified at the thought of trying to uncover the news; they prefer to worry. Here are some good ways of dealing with the possibility of cancer in your future:

- Accept that you may indeed be diagnosed with cancer someday.
- Remind yourself that everyone dies of something.
- Stay abreast of information on treatments for the type of cancer that runs in your family.
- Have periodic screenings that will help catch cancer early.
- Figure out how you'll deal with cancer. Then, set the subject on the back burner of your consciousness. Promise yourself to spend no more time fretting about something that may or may not happen. Otherwise, you're extending the length of time you must deal with it.

You're experiencing horrible anxiety over the death of a beloved pet

Your pet may have been your best friend—always there, never judgmental, totally loyal. No wonder you loved Fluffy so much!

So, the loss of a beloved pet can feel very much like the loss of a child or any other loved one. Dealing with it is difficult. Here are some ideas for handling your period of bereavement:

- Share your feeling with a fellow pet lover. Don't cry on the shoulder of someone who doesn't understand animal-human love stories.
- Do something to memorialize your pet. Set up a photo shrine in a room of your house. Tuck her pink-leather collar away in your treasure box. Find a way to commemorate the role she played in your life—and the fine contribution she made.

- Give yourself permission to mourn and be miserable, but set a deadline. You can't allow yourself to be steeped in misery forever; remember, that isn't the "you" that the pet adored and followed so loyally.
- Reminisce about things you loved—again, with someone who has a pet or has had one in the past.
- Don't expect to get over it quickly.
- Be calmed by knowing that all the love your pet gave so generously is still with you. Remember your pet and special moments spent together, and the love will come flowing back and give you happiness and comfort.

You obsess about old grievances and grudges

You have a list of all the people who have done you wrong. And that, in itself, is fairly benign. What's not productive is turning to the list often, and with anger.

Let the act of list-making serve as a way of putting the anger behind you, not a way of puffing it up. This is one anxiety-maker that you can easily dismantle, if you're willing to face that some matters never get settled. That's okay. Letting the old evil push your hot buttons means you experience the hurt over and over again. Don't allow old issues to interfere with today's peace.

Do what you can to stop yourself. Perhaps you need to perform a "burial" of the list in your fireplace, putting it away once and for all. When you think of the past—and feel panic rising up—breathe deeply for several minutes. Turn to your Sun Scene and visualize yourself there, free of all anxiety.

You want to have a baby, but your mate doesn't want children

Obviously, having children or not having children should be discussed prior to marriage. However, because that obviously wasn't the case in your situation, you need to leave the marriage to pursue your dream...or stay and relegate your dream to the realm of things you wanted to do, but didn't. The latter can be a heartrending regret when you're 45 and wishing you'd never given in to your mate's strong feelings on the subject. The resentment can be a huge source of ongoing anxiety.

So, the key here is resolution, here and now. You may need counseling to hash out this subject. For the time being, though, make your needs clear to your mate and if you know that his or her mind is set, do some soul-searching and then make your decision. Otherwise, you'll live with anxiety for the rest of your life—and this is one of the rawest wounds a person can have.

Remember that single people can adopt (so you don't have to let your decision hinge on the thought that you'll never find another mate).

Remember that you probably can love someone other than the one you're with.

Remember that a resentment-based relationship only gets worse.

You moved to a new house and experienced anxiety over the change

After a move, you may feel conflicted about the decision to change residences: "Will I be able to afford the payment? Is it too far from my work (or my child's school)?" The list goes on and on.

But you moved. And if it turns out that the rent or payment is too high, it's too far, or whatever the problem might be, that can be resolved. And if necessary, you can move again. You're not bound to a mistake forever, even though moving is so stressful that it can sometimes feel that way.

When panic hits, calm yourself with the skills described in Chapter 3, and don't beat yourself up about bad decisions. Decide what you can do if the move doesn't work out as expected. Then, leave the subject alone.

You're facing the threat of jail, or you're in prison

This is one situation in which you can look at the worst-case scenario—the old "what's the worst thing that could happen"—and not get much reassurance. Nonetheless, you need to do it.

Make yourself look at what you would actually do if the worst eventuality came true. What would you do if you got a jail sentence? Would you die? Would all your friends and relatives desert you? In truth, people have gone to jail, and they have lived. Some find ways to make lemonade of their lemon years.

One Houston doctor sentenced to 20 years in prison used the time to read every book in the prison library—and to teach other inmates to read. He took an awful life detour and simply made the best of it.

Get your arms around what you'll do if they handcuff you and take you away to jail. Then, even though you'll be upset if that happens, you won't be unprepared.

You have dieting and appearance anxiety

It's a material, visual world we live in, and none of us gets away from that—not if we walk outside our homes. So, if you feel anxiety over style and clothing and weight, consider the following ways to lift yourself out of the weight/appearance doldrums:

- Decide if you'd like to make changes and figure out how. *Get with the Program!* by Bob Greene, presents a nutritionally sound lifestyle that works. If your food plan is something you "go on" and then resume old eating ways, you'll always be doing the yo-yo weight loss/gain.
- Hire a personal shopper who comes highly recommended to guide you in discovering what looks best on you. Men who don't have a woman in the house can enjoy this option just as much as women; usually, a shopper will show a man a wardrobe that's a bit more fashion-forward than his current brown/black staples.
- Go to a salon in your city and splurge on a makeover. Many women make the mistake of sticking with makeup and hairstyle that worked for them 20 years earlier but isn't "getting it done" anymore.
- Stop using self-putdowns. Hold your head and chin high; work for better posture and think confident.

- Emulate a person you think is great to be around—try this person's socializing skills. Does he or she ask questions about others? Does this person smile a lot?
- Enjoy every day—make the most of it, and show compassion and kindness to people everywhere you go.
- Don't listen to naysayers. If you have a mate or a friend who tells you "that's not going to work" or "you don't have what it takes," look around for people who are encouraging.
- Once you've come up with plans for your weight and your appearance, be happy with what you've chosen. Don't let others persuade you to set different goals. It's your look, not theirs. Be satisfied with the way you are.
- Give smiles away flagrantly and extravagantly—they're free.

You have infertility anxiety

At age 36 (or almost 45 in your mind), you fret constantly about "When will I have a baby?" "Will I have a baby?" or "What if I never have a baby?" You've taken a perfectly lovely part of life and transformed it into a source of anxiety. Why not try doing something different, such as the following:

- If you're married and trying to get pregnant, give yourself and your mate a break, especially if you've already gone the infertility-test route. You're here on earth to enjoy life and do things for others, and moaning 24-hours-a-day about not having a baby isn't endearing. Do fun, relaxing things, and visualize yourself having a good life. Count your blessings.
- If you're married and your mate doesn't want children, you have a major decision to make. Are you going to persuade your mate—or is this refusal a deal-breaker?
- If you're not dating anyone, don't let your ticking biological clock cause you to grab someone—anyone—and wrap this person up in good qualities that aren't there, in order for this man to be marriage-worthy. The best mates for most of us are found through dating slowly but surely and assessing mutual interests, values, and goals.

You obsess about violence in the world today

The events of September 11, 2001, redefined our world. For some, this led to a fear of leaving home, a fear of opening mail, or a fear of being in a public arena or tall building. Coping mechanisms had to be relearned, and grieving processes seemed never-ending. But for most Americans, the option of not resolving the anxiety did not exist, because life circumstances required getting on with earning a living and taking care of families.

But what if you haven't been able to shake your preoccupation with safety issues? Feeling fearful is not abnormal. But work on revamping your viewpoint so that you can still be passionate about living. Try the following:

- Consider the likelihood of your being attacked or targeted. If you're in public service, your risk is far greater, probably, than someone who is a teacher or grocery-store owner. Be realistic about your risk factor, be it high or low. Have a sense of humor about it: "Yes, I'm sure Osama Bin Laden is saying, 'Okay, the Women's Poetry Society in Conroe, Texas, is next on our list.'"

- Ramp up your gutsiness. Firefighters did not enter the World Trade Center buildings with hesitation, and you can't enter each day in a tentative, fearful way. You, and others, can honor the memory of these heroes by living full-throttle. Resolve to live fully and fear minimally.

- Don't give in to the cocooning effect. When you feel yourself wanting to stay at home and cower in bed, that just means you want to control your environment. The problem is, living in a paralyzed state just fulfills all the world terrorists' dream for Americans. They want to see our quality of living compromised. But if you look at history—and the hardships endured by our predecessors—you won't let yourself give in to irrational fears.

- Let rational wariness guide you: If that means buying antibiotics to gird yourself and feel prepared, do it. If you want to stock up on food and water, that's also fine.

- Accept that life is different now, no matter how often you say that you want things back the way they were.
- Get information you need. Do you know where you would go to the emergency room if you needed to? Do you know the best way to handle an injury? Are you alert?
- Don't let yourself focus on death and destruction. Turn your thoughts to positive things: what you can do for the unfortunate, how you can show your love to family and friends, how lucky you are to be alive.
- Develop a routine that is action-oriented; get yourself out there, moving, doing, helping, and sharing. Many people reassessed how they were living in the wake of September 11, and much of America agreed that this was a "benefit" of the horrible tragedy. Although we hated what happened, it made us examine how we were spending our days. Before that, maybe your plan was to have fun "someday"—after you were through putting in 15-hour days. Or you would switch to the kind of work you really want to do after five years of doing something you hate. Or you would spend time with your child after you satisfied your hunger for fame and fortune. Overnight, we all learned to say and do what matters—today.
- Clear your mind of cobwebs; pray and meditate. Dilute your fears by strengthening your spirituality. If you need to grieve for years for those who died September 11, do so; just don't let it become a reason to hide.
- Let 9-11 make you better. If the person you were prior to September 11 was just going through the motions, imagine that you're living vicariously for one of the souls lost in the tragedy. Give your family affection like that person would if he could. Relish children and sunshine just like that person would if he had gotten a chance to live longer.

If your anxiety is so debilitating that you can't go to work or be with loved ones or do anything productive, **seek help from a medical professional.**

You worry about personal safety precautions

As mentioned in the entry above, do whatever it takes to feel secure. It is all right to have extra locks and weapons and mace. It is not all right, however, to go in your bedroom and hibernate for the rest of your natural days. If you try the suggestions listed on page 211 for reframing your fears and they fail to work, **you probably need counseling.**

You worry about getting housework done along with working full-time

You just can't seem to get everything done. You fret and worry, and sometimes the panic just wells up inside you in a frightening way. And this is not a problem most people can empathize with. They probably just think you're silly to be obsessing over nothing.

One of the best skills for dealing with this problem is thought-stopping. When you start beating yourself up about your domestic failures, simply say "stop it." Turn to something that will make you laugh—a joke someone e-mailed you, a sitcom rerun, anything to remove you from that serious frame of mind.

If you obsess about a clean house and compulsively keep it spotless, seek counseling when you find that this is interfering with relationships (as in, bothering your mate or kids).

You're reeling from having had a traffic accident or minor law violation

You had an encounter with law enforcement, which is enough to give almost anyone anxiety. You have the right to feel anxious—it's a natural response to a traffic accident or a minor law violation.

Take care of the logical steps: getting information on the other driver (insurance, driver's license). Then, when you get home, talk it over with someone you're close to. No one is going to kill you, and it's not likely you'll end up in prison. Tell yourself: "I can deal with this. I will be positive, and I'll do what it takes to put this behind me."

Avoiding it, or constantly reliving it, will only make you feel worse.

Crazy drivers make you anxious

In traffic, you go nuts. You shout at other drivers from inside your car. You give them dirty looks. You are well-versed in obscene gestures.

But all of these skills get you nothing but a higher level of frustration and anxiety. So, because what you're doing isn't working, how about trying something different? Be the guru of peacefulness. Mother Teresa. The Sultan of Goodwill. Take your pick.

Sample a new mantra for the road: "I wish these people well, even the radical drivers. I hope they get to their destinations safely. I'm not in a race with them; I won't follow too closely, gesture madly, or in any way make their day worse. I will be the positive force on the highway today."

Your fears are causing you to indulge in obsessive behaviors

You keep double-checking to make sure you turned off all the burners, the oven, or the lights. You can't reassure yourself enough times that your doors are locked or that your hands are clean. Some people even have obsessive thoughts, such as, "I'm going to stab my mate" or "I'm going to toss myself off the side of the freeway."

Remember that the gap between entertaining a thought and actually doing it is enormous. The likelihood of translating these things into action is practically nil. But you can practice the following to deal more effectively with obsessive behaviors:

- Jot down your behaviors that you feel driven to do.
- Confront what could be causing you to do these (fear of a house fire, fear of losing control, and so forth).
- Find a new response to use when that certain fear flies into your mind. When you panic because you want to recheck to

see if the door is locked, clasp your hands, look skyward, and visit your Sun Scene on a private beach. There, you free yourself of the need to double-check compulsively. There, you are more serene, and less worried. (And...you're getting a tan.)

- Think of what you fear, and do something different in response to it. Do this many times each day.

You're anxious over your new role as a retiree or graduate

Many negative thoughts may go through your mind, and most of these probably involve doubts about abilities to handle your new situation well. Decompress and say: "I'll look at this as a major opportunity—a new phase in my life that will have wonderful aspects to it."

- Decide what you would like to do that you now can do because you are a retiree or graduate.
- Jot down goals.
- Join a group—retirees who travel, or new Baptist kids on campus.
- Keep ratcheting up your enthusiasm for this new part of your life—strange, scary, and full of excitement.

You're afraid of flying

Even though a great deal of time has passed since 9-11, many Americans feel very shaky about flying. What was once referred to simply as "fear of flying" has escalated into full-fledged phobias.

Here are some guidelines for coping with flying fears:

- Acknowledge that you feel afraid and that this is natural—not "odd."
- When the plane is taking off, use a relaxation technique. Breathe deeply and close your eyes. Meditate or pray. Or imagine yourself with all the other passengers as you get off the plane, after having reached your destination safely.

- Don't be surprised if your heart thumps harder as the plane takes off or lands. You're nervous and that's okay.
- Think happy thoughts—silly as that sounds, there's something magical about listing "favorite things."
- Use thought-stopping if your mind finds its way to 9-11 visuals, or starts listing all the things that could go wrong with the plane itself, human error, or terrorist strike. Replace that thinking with something good you've seen—your child running up to meet you with a handful of wildflowers she picked, for example.
- Accept your lack of control. Your fears may revolve around the possibility of a crash or being trapped inside the plane, but either way, you must turn over the controls to the pilot. Send the pilot your best wishes for a very good flying day.
- Try reverse psychology. "Oh, well, if it happens today, I've had a good life—I've got to die sometime." The idea is that in relinquishing your fear of dying, you're handing over the reins to a higher power (or fate).
- Focus on what you'll do when you reach the next town. Jot down a list of plans, must-sees, calls to make, and so forth. Take yourself to a different orbit.

You're plagued by worries about natural disasters

Anxiety about disasters (floods, fires, and so forth) can make you jumpy, agitated, and anxiety-ridden. If you can't seem to shake your nervousness, try some of these coping skills:

- Keep a routine to your life that gets you out of the house. If your doldrums make you come up with excuses why you can't go places, set yourself up for not being able to refuse. For example, if you don't want to miss your volunteer work now that you've signed up, but you worry about driving in the rain because of the potential for flooding, have your car loaded to the gills with clothes donations that you need to drop off on your volunteer day...otherwise, you can't even go to buy groceries because there's no room for grocery sacks the car's so jam-packed with clothes. It may sound convoluted but it works.

- Use the desensitization method—gradual exposures to decrease your fears about floods, fires, or whatever, by unraveling your fear and looking at its likelihood of occurring. For example, drive when it's raining so that you gradually work yourself up to forging street streams. (Elsewhere in this book, see the full description of desensitizing to fears of rising water.)
- Read everything you can find on the fear of disasters so that you grow your understanding of it. With greater education comes reduced fear.
- See disaster movies in order to desensitize yourself.
- Don't drink more than a cup of coffee and one cola a day. Keep your alcohol intake low.
- Reach out. Support your sister whose son has cancer; your friend whose father died last month; or another friend who can't talk because of a stroke.
- Rest. When you're plagued by scary nightmares, try to wake up and restart your sleep pattern with calm thoughts.
- Be honest with yourself about fearing disasters. Work on ridding yourself of these fears.

You have an extreme fear of driving a car

To get rid of a fear of driving, try thought-stopping and exposing yourself to the problem and changing your responses to this cue. Reporting on how to handle driving phobia, *The Journal of Behavior Therapy and Experimental Psychiatry* (September-December 2000) showed the effectiveness of virtual reality exposure therapy (VRET). After a week to establish a baseline, the patients had three sessions of treatment during a 10-day period. This included practicing four virtual reality (VR) driving scenarios. Peak anxiety decreased in sessions and ratings of anxiety and avoidance went down. In addition, these gains were still in evidence at a seven-month followup. Researchers concluded that VRET should be tested in controlled clinical trials to see if the finding holds up.

You feel anxious over the idea of any form of stressful conversation

Some people avoid stressful conversations at all costs. Fearful of the anxiety that is attached, they dodge the issues, appease difficult people, and smooth over hostilities, all of which worsen the original problem or weaken the relationship.

You can rehearse conversations that you think will be difficult, in order to tweak your wording and tone. You're less likely to be thrown off balance if you have a few phrases ready. Learn from the past—know the people and the kinds of talks that have proven stressful in the past, and prepare your conversational approaches.

You have an eating disorder

Our society sets people up for eating disorders. If you're one of these individuals, you know all too well that high-level anxiety is a part of that unpretty picture. You feel stressed about your appearance, so you eat too much and gain weight and make things worse.

Or you worry because you don't look like a reed-thin model, so you starve yourself and get a wan, sickly appearance for your trouble. Many people spend most of their lives yo-yo dieting; they gain weight, lose weight, and then gain more back.

Some people binge and purge. They ruin their teeth with devastating vomiting. Some folks are so anxiety-filled that they grind their teeth down all night long during sleep.

You need to seek treatment from an eating-disorders specialist at a clinic that deals with these problems routinely; this is essential. And you can also try the following self-help tips for changing eating-disordered ways:

- Set up one goal (and it's not a specific weight). You want to develop healthy attitudes about food. You've lived too long equating weight gain with being bad and weight loss with being good. It hasn't worked. (Who wants to be good all the time?) Think of food as an enjoyable part of life, but not a prime focus. Meals fuel your body.

- Try grazing. At first blush, it may sound scary: "If I eat a number of small meals throughout the day, won't I gain weight big time?" No, because most people who do this are also trying to improve their diet, including more fresh produce and healthy snacks. Better eating becomes part of your life— not a diet you go on.
- Keep track of what you eat and why. If you eat out of boredom or because you're mad, jot that down.
- Don't let anyone put you on a diet. Learn about eating healthy: nutrition for maximum performance, tips for eating out, etc. Get smart about food.
- Think of things you can do when you're tempted to pig out. "The next time I want to dig into the cookie bag, I'll go repot some plants."
- Don't beat yourself up for having a piece of chocolate pie at your aunt's house. If you deprive yourself of all the things you love, you'll never like your new plan. You have to like it to make it a way of life.
- Weigh yourself every other day. People lie to themselves. They fib to themselves when they look in the mirror, and when pants get tight, they blame the cleaners for shrinking them. To keep your weight from getting out of control, keep tabs on it. Don't do it in a maniacal kind of way. Just track your weight to stay healthy. And don't interpret a slight gain as a life-or-death predictor of how you're doing. Food is fuel and you're checking to see if you're overfueling.

When patients have anxiety disorders along with eating disorders, treating the anxiety problem concurrently can help to prove the outcome.

You're filled with anxiety because your baby cries often

Crying baby/anxiety-ridden mother—a "which came first: chicken or egg" kind of question. However, a study reported in *Child Care Health Development* (September 1998) documents that babies who cry often and excessively are usually in the hands of mothers who are depressed, filled with anxiety, exhausted, angry, and distressed about their marriages.

This means these moms must tone down their anxiety to be in a position to calm their babies. Infants pick up on discontent and anxiety in their mothers and show their discomfiture by crying.

A mother dealing with high levels of anxiety can use some of the anxiety-curbing skills in Chapter 3, such as changing responses to cues and thought-stopping.

You're living with a sexually transmitted disease, such as HIV or genital herpes

Herpes and HIV won't go away—both are lifelong problems—so you must learn to adapt so that STD-driven anxiety isn't a part of your every day.

Assuming that you have already seen a doctor and you're receiving appropriate treatment, you may want to try the following ways of dealing with your disease:

- Reframe the poor-me script that runs through your head when you think of your sexually transmitted disease (STD). Promise yourself that instead of letting your STD define you, you will pursue your goals despite the disease.
- Deal with anxiety by making lists of things to do each day.
- When negative thoughts bother you, challenge them. When you tell yourself "nobody will want to date me," look at that distortion of the truth. Maybe some people won't want to date you, but this isn't every single person. Furthermore, some people wouldn't want to date you just because they don't like redheads, and you're a redhead, or whatever.
- Stay active. The more you're out doing things—taking exercise classes, going to church, meeting people—the less time you will have for sadness.
- Do things to help others. Contributing will make you less focused on your own predicament. There's nothing like volunteer work to take the emphasis off you and put it on someone who probably has more problems than you do.

11

Curbing the Anxiety of Money Troubles

Anxiety-Busting Tools for This Chapter:

- Thought-stopping.
- Changing responses to cues.
- Relationship-building.

You're having a lot of anxiety over your inability to save money

TO INGRAIN A NEW HABIT, MAKE IT A PRIORITY. THEN, DO SOMETHING to effect change. In this case, pay yourself first every time you get a paycheck. You'll be forced to live on what's left. Even if you're only putting aside $100 a month, you will develop a savings habit. Over the years, increase the amount and you'll be looking at some terrific savings.

When you feel anxious that you're not saving enough, give yourself a break. This mental cue just makes you feel bad. When your brain brings out that whip, tell yourself, "I'm saving enough for right now. Go away, guilt. I don't want to hang with you."

You feel anxious about your stock-market losses

Make the wrong calls in the stock market, and you may get anxious feelings that you're a screwup. This can eat at your peace of mind until you're constantly on edge. Are you waiting for someone to punish you for your mistakes?

Try other approaches. As one teen told her mother who had lost $100,000 on a bad investment, "Just make some more money, and you can replace what you lost."

Look at the past as history. Today is opportunity. Tomorrow is a dream. And mold that into a good financial picture. There is no way that castigating yourself for past mistakes will put coins in your purse.

Decide what you want and how you're going to get it. Take steps to make something happen. Don't be tripped up by self-doubt.

You're stressed by loss of money in a failed business venture

Kick yourself one more time, and you'll have absolutely nothing left to sit on. Entrepreneurs who lose money in a venture often have trouble seeing the future because they're too busy looking back and rerunning history (with improvements, of course). Truth is, nothing will alter the fact that your business failed. That doesn't make you a failure and it doesn't predict what's ahead. As long as you still have your mind and healthy body and skills and work ethic, you can do some amazing things.

Tuck these survival skills into your power-pack: thought-stopping, changing responses to cues, and learning to avoid blame-shifting.

You worry that your retirement funds aren't sufficient

Looking at your portfolio gives you anxiety. What seemed like what would be enough 20 years ago now seems woefully lame. You figure that, optimistically, if you eat one meal a day and never drive your car or spend a dime on entertainment, you can eke out a retirement existence.

Why not look for other solutions? Plenty of semi-retired people take on part-time jobs as consultants in their fields—or do something entirely new. With the cushion of a little extra income, you'll feel less anxious.

You're experiencing litigation stress

Just seeing the return address of an attorney on an envelope gives you chills. You've been sued, you're going to mediation soon, and that's all you can think about. Your throat dries up, your chest hurts, and you feel exhausted.

Coping with a difficult time in your life requires reframing the awfulness of what's going on. Yes, you're miserable and worried, but this isn't the end of your life. If you've hired an attorney who is handling the matter, do everything you can to thought-stop each time you feel a rush of anxiety. Imagine yourself placing the problem in his "professional" arms.

Also, try using these skills (from Chapter 3):

- Changing responses to cues.
- Role-playing/visualization.
- Inoculating against stressors.

One of the most helpful things you can do is to visualize yourself walking away from mediation day with the problem resolved. Your anxiety is behind you. The litigation is over, and you're getting on with your life. Imagine the exhilaration, the joy of shedding the stress, as your shoulders relax, finally freed of that heavy worry and sense of responsibility that you've been carrying around.

You had a reversal of fortune, foreclosure, or repossession

You are totally deflated. You keep looking back so much of the time that it's almost impossible to look ahead. You can't work and your personal relationships are suffering. So, is hand-wringing making things better?

If not, try the following:

- List the things that are all right in your life—perhaps even good.
- Ask yourself if it's somewhat gratifying that you have some joy in your life.
- Do what you can to decrease the downsides of the reversal of fortune, foreclosure, or repossession. Then, find closure by telling yourself, "I have done all that I can do."
- When you revisit your disappointment, stop. Shake your head and say, "I'm not going to do that. I'll play solitaire, or take my dog for a walk." Have a plan to draw yourself out of the doldrums.

The IRS is pursuing you

They want you to pay up. You owe money from a failed business venture in which payroll taxes weren't paid. You have good reason to be looking over your shoulder.

What you can do is hire a tax attorney. Explain the situation, and ask if he would advise you to meet with the IRS and work out a plan. Once you've gotten some advice, put the subject away—it's being handled. You're not an expert in taxes (obviously), so rely on your tax professional's advice. When the subject comes to your mind again, replay the same message.

You feel growing money distress with no hope in sight

Tension between couples can result from money difficulties. Or you may be facing financial disaster all alone. Perhaps, your spending or gambling got you in a fix. Or it could have been something beyond your control, such as job loss or business failure. But you can take the following proactive moves to improve matters:

- Promise yourself to quit worrying and start doing something about your mess.
- Make a written list of obligations you have, and figure out how to pay something on each debt each month, even if it's only 10 dollars. Contact each creditor and explain your plan. Don't worry if they yell at you or say it's not enough. Just stick with your plan. Doing something is better than nothing.
- If the situation is terribly daunting (you couldn't pay off your debts in this lifetime), see a bankruptcy lawyer. Most cities have attorneys who do pro bono work, so check with the local bar association.
- Have a plan for paying off your credit cards and the people you owe money.
- Be matter-of-fact. "This is the situation I'm in, and here's what I can do. I'm through hating myself, and I'm on to doing something."

12

Now What?
(Alternative Options)

You've tried modifying your behavior, but you're still having anxiety and/or panic attacks.

So, maybe, you need to tack on a touch of the unorthodox. Buy a Harry Potter book, or get a cute kitschy Barbie fountain pen and write in a hot-pink diary. Kid stuff for grownups has become trendy, as people seek to smudge reality somewhat—but in an innocent, drug-free way. Women are decorating their limbs with temporary tattoos. Guys unwind on PlayStation 2. Stars like Julia Roberts are taking up knitting, and calling it the "new yoga." Obviously, these fanciful endeavors won't get rid of panic attacks, but they can provide you with lighthearted fun and help you relax.

As Bernadette Murphy says in her new book *Zen and the Art of Knitting*, needlework can bring on a relaxation response, complete with lowered blood pressure and heart rate. In fact, any repetitive activity brings on a meditative state in the brain. Your neurons cross their legs and settle down for a little decompression time.

Today, you can even add to your entourage a person called a "stress-reduction trainer," who can tutor you in t'ai chi, meditation, or another type of relaxation technique.

Some people are most comfortable with anxiety-busting instruction that's person-to-person, and this is especially true in an era when it's easy to isolate oneself and exist behind the tentacles of e-mail, voice mail, and faxing. Do, however, be a wary consumer. Just because you want a sounding board doesn't mean you should swap proven treatments for a feeling of being understood.

Anxiety and panic attacks can be serious, so watch out for people who may be out to defraud you with false, overblown healing claims. Sometimes, even swindlers think they have good intentions, and can come off as extremely concerned about your problems.

Going the alternative route

Before you take the paths less traveled—alternative medicine (also called complementary medicine)—be aware that this category usually features therapies that aren't used in hospitals routinely, and thus, aren't reimbursed by insurance companies. Some people still want to try these because some people do benefit from using holistic (whole-person-oriented) therapies in addition to conventional treatments for anxiety.

Before you try an alternative therapy under the direction of a mentor, examine that person's credentials and get satisfied-client testimonials. Most importantly, discuss all treatments and therapies with your physician. Your doctor can tell you if what you're about to try could be detrimental to your health. The fact that alternative healthcare givers do not attend medical school should be a red flag that says to proceed with caution.

Avoid signing long-term agreements. An ethical professional will not need guarantees that you're coming back for more. Also, be wary of fees that seem over-the-top. Watch out for control-freak health advisors who tell you, "Turn yourself over to me, do what I say, and you'll be fine."

Doing the New Age thing

When you learned anxiety-busting skills (Chapter 3), you delved into the area of mind-body healing approaches. Other options are yoga, art therapy, dance therapy, meditation, hypnosis, and music therapy, most of which are taught at holistic-health centers, as well as other facilities.

Alternatives that help some individuals rid themselves of anxiety also include: acupuncture, herbal supplements, t'ai chi, massage, reflexology, Pilates, and biofeedback. Many bodywork centers offer, along with full rosters of massage, the Japanese technique of Reiki, which features the "laying on of hands" for reducing stress. Spiritually guided life-force energy is believed to treat the physical, emotional, mental, and spiritual. Another form of bodywork, therapeutic touch, is said to promote relaxation and reduce anxiety.

Mind-healing through meditation

Find a quiet spot and experiment with mindful banishing of stress and anxiety. If you dislike the idea of being passive physically during mind-relaxation, try the active meditation called t'ai chi. Visualization is another way to "settle down." You imagine yourself whisking away fears. You can even use an audiotape to take you through the steps of self-hypnosis.

Don't be surprised if your first attempts are herky-jerky. You're not used to allowing yourself such a downtime from activity, so you have to give yourself permission to take timeout—repeatedly if necessary. You're entitled to a peaceful respite, and you'll probably get to the point that you look forward to moving into that quiet spot set aside for deep-breathing and slow-feeling.

Turn off your mind and its mad dashing, so that you can be totally in the moment—feeling, experiencing, and relaxing. Enter a calming state in which you mindfully appreciate life, and feel a sense of compassion for all living things, leaving behind your buzzing brain. Forgive all, fear not, and open your senses to everything around you.

You should feel better after practicing meditation, especially after you get used to the idea that taking time out for personal growth is really, truly all right. Give it 5 to 15 minutes a day—or more.

Taking t'ai chi up a few levels

Some people like to t'ai chi their way past anxiety. Soldiers once used the martial art of t'ai chi chuan. Today, many people become aficionados by taking classes or using videotapes that teach the many movements and postures. As is true of any sport or exercise, having a professional teach you is a good launching pad for success. That way, you don't have to "unlearn" bad habits and you're less likely to hurt yourself. The special ways to breathe and "circulate energy" are hard to get the hang of without an instructor.

Detoxifying your body

Maybe you saw the movie *L.A. Story*, in which Sarah Jessica Parker persuades Steve Martin that he needs a "cleansing," and leads him on a colonics caper. Well, that's one way of detoxifying—some hate it, others love it. But, you can also sample a less radical route of detoxifying—and that's by eliminating caffeine, nicotine, and alcohol, none of which adds anything to your serenity.

Of course, you shouldn't go cold turkey on all three at the same time. Wean yourself off alcohol and smoking. Then, work on tapering off of caffeine. However, be prepared for withdrawal headaches, especially if you taper too quickly. You may want to get your physician's advice on handling the physical symptoms you'll experience when leaving behind all three of these things.

Change your everyday patterns so that eliminating caffeine, nicotine, and alcohol feels less jarring. Doing things differently can smooth the transition to a brand-new detoxified body. Find a support program or counselor if you need help.

Self-helping your way to a great relationship

Eliminating thorns in your relationship with your mate may require some intensive work. This area doesn't get better overnight, but if you're willing to devote time to improving matters, you can make huge strides.

Two self-help books that can pave your way to success are: Phil McGraw's *Relationship Rescue*—and a book co-authored by Diane Stafford (one of the authors of *No More Panic Attacks*). It's titled *Close Encounters: 100 Tips for Achieving the Intimacy You Desire* (available on Amazon, by authors Cari La Grange, Dr. Marvin Stone, and Diane Stafford).

Wake up and smell sweet scent-sations

Ever try aromatherapy for calming? Some people swear by aromatic inhalers called "whiffers." These are small devices that look like fountain pens that contain essential oils: rose geranium, peppermint, orange/grapefruit, lavender, eucalyptus, among others. You hold one of these under your nose and breathe in the fragrance. Combine with daily affirmations at moments of high anxiety, and see if it soothes. (Available online at *www.sacredcurrents.com*.) This Website also sells feng shui candles and aromatherapy lockets.

Herbal remedies

Some people swear by herbal supplements for reducing anxiety, although many medical experts don't consider these worthwhile. Most physicians take a wait-and-see approach, but don't recommend these to patients because of the lack of studies validating their efficacy.

Take advertising hype into consideration when making decisions about using alternative treatments for anxiety. Since prescriptions are not required for the use of herbal supplements, some are marketed with wild promises.

Before taking supplements, check with your doctor, who knows your medical history, health status, and medications. Your doctor can advise you about any adverse interactions.

If you're going to use herbs for anxiety, consider the following:

Passionflower

Sometimes used as a sedative due to its anti-anxiety effect, passionflower can be combined with valerian to relieve insomnia and anxiety. Dosage for anxiety: one dropperful in warm water, or one capsule of dried plant. Dosage for sleep improvement: 200-300 mg of the extract, an hour before going to bed.

St. John's wort

This is used for moderate depression accompanied by anxiety. Though not studied specifically for anxiety disorders, this may be better than valerian in that it represents stronger science. Downside: interactions with other drugs. Recommended dosage: 300 mg of 0.3-percent hypericin extract in three divided doses. Use four to six weeks. If you see no improvement, discontinue. Side effect is constipation. Those who have severe depression, bipolar disorder, or suicidal ideation should **not** use St. John's wort and should be evaluated by a physician. Also, don't use St. John's wort if you're on amphetamines, narcotics, amino acids, diet pills, asthma inhalants, hay fever medications, antidepressants, over-the-counter cold products, or if you're pregnant or breastfeeding.

Valerian

Although some evidence exists that valerian acts as a tranquilizer, offering a sedative-hypnotic effect, no thorough studies verify this. Recommended dose is 2 to 3 g of the dried root (prepared by steeping without boiling). Occasionally, people using valerian have reported gastrointestinal complaints and contact allergies. As a depressant, this should not be taken on a long-term basis.

Note: By the way, put the herb **kava-kava** on your list of things *not* to try. Once thought to be safe for quelling anxiety, kava was nixed on March 26, 2002, when the FDA issued a warning to consumers that kava-containing supplements have been linked to liver-related injuries.

• • •

The more things you try, the more likely you are to zero in on exactly what works for you. Remember, you have a whole spectrum of options, from the frivolous (toys and gadgets) to the fringe (herbal supplements) to the fixer-uppers (coping skills and changing your behavior) to the nitty-gritty neuron-soothers (drug-therapy).

...And, you can always Net-work

If you're a self-helper with computer skills, check out the following Websites that offer tips, support groups, and resources for those who suffer from panic and anxiety (we also include phone numbers for low-tech types):

American Psychiatric Association: *www.psych.org*
(202) 682-6220

Anxiety Disorders Association of America: *www.adaa.org*
(301) 231-9350

National Anxiety Foundation
(606) 272-7166

National Institute of Mental Health: *www.nimh.nih.gov*
(301) 443-5258

National Mental Health Association: *www.nmha.org*
(800) 969-NMHA

National Mental Health Consumers' Self-Help: (800) 553-4539

National Self-Help Clearinghouse: *selfhelpweb.org*
(212) 354-8525

Obsessive Compulsive Foundation: (203) 878-5669

Panic and Other Anxiety Disorders: (800) 647-2642

Panic Disorders Online:
Panicdisorder.about.com/health/panicdisorder

Phobics Anonymous: (619) 322-COPE

Social Anxiety Support: *www.socialanxietysupport.com*

Society for Traumatic Stress Studies: (708) 480-9080

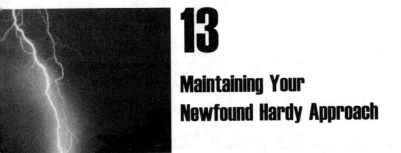

13

Maintaining Your Newfound Hardy Approach

WITH NEW SKILLS IN TOW, YOU MAY NEVER HAVE TO EXPERIENCE PANIC attacks again, hopefully. But healthy living has no down side, so even if you no longer worry about panic attacks, you should hedge your bets with the following maintenance plan:

1. Continue to work on your newly acquired skills and try to use them regularly (Chapter 3)

If you have an anxious friend, share your coping skills. These days, you won't have to look far to find an anxious person.

2. Continue growing your physical awareness

Get enough rest, eat healthy, and exercise. Take walks; enjoy nature. Every day make a point of appreciating the uniqueness of another human being.

3. Volunteer

Keep helping the group you signed up for during exercises in the 30-day plan, or find another. Donate a few hours each week. The joy of giving will come back to you 10-fold.

4. Be realistic

Know what kinds of things increase your anxiety, and then, don't make things worse for yourself.

5. If you have another panic attack, don't let the misstep ruin your momentum

You know how to manage anxiety, but you may never be *cured.* But, if you can handle panic and anxiety effectively most of the time, you are 99 percent there.

6. Be patient

Understand that friends and relatives who've never experienced panic attacks have a tendency to tell you to "get a grip" or "you *could* get better if you tried." Of course, what we know (and they fail to comprehend) is that if it were that easy, millions of people would not be plagued by anxiety every day.

7. Go to bed and get up at similar times every day

Having a routine is a good thing. And keeping your mind free of negatives is even better. When you catch yourself obsessing about something awful that might happen later in the day, tonight, or tomorrow, say "wait—stop." Work on today and only today. Stop your mind from sabotaging your growth.

Lots of people are having a wonderful time living on this earth. You're going to be one of them!

Bibliography

"A Journey to Recovery from Anxiety Disorders." Anxiety Disorders Association of America Website.
www.adaa.org/aboutanxietydisorders/journeytorecovery.

"An Introduction to Phobias." DrKoop.com Website.
www.drkoop.com.

"Anxiety Disorders." American Psychiatric Association Website.
www.psych.org/public_info/anxiety.cfm.

"Anxiety Disorders." National Institute of Mental Health.
www.nimh.nih.gov/anxiety/anxiety/index.htm.

"Anxiety Disorders." The Body Website. National Institute of Mental Health, National Institutes of Health.
www.thebody.com/nimh/anxiety.html.

American Psychiatric Association. *Diagnostic Criteria from DSM-IV.* Washington, D.C.: American Psychiatric Association, 1994.

Ballenger, James; Newman, Cory; Ross, Jerilyn; and Schwartz, Stephen L. "Social Phobia: More Prevalent Than You Think." *Patient Care 33* (August 15, 1999):120-130.

Ballenger, J.C.; Davidson, J.R.; Lecrubier, Y.; Nutt, D.J.; Borkovec, T.D.; Rickel, K.; Stein, D.J.; and Wittchen, H.U. "Consensus Statement on Generalized Anxiety Disorder from the International Consensus Group on Depression and Anxiety." *Journal of Clinical Psychiatry* 33 (August 2001):53-8. *www.ncbi.nlm.nih.gov.*

Bates, Betsy. "Hypnosis Reduced Surgical Cost, Time, and Anxiety." *Family Practice News 30* (March 1, 2000):16a.

Battaglia, M.; Bertella, S; Politi, E.; Bernardeschi, L.; Perna, G.; Gabriele, A.; and Bellodi, L. "Age at Onset of Panic Disorder: Influence of Familial Liability to the Disease and of Childhood Separation Disorder." *American Journal of Psychiatry* 152 (1995):1362-4. *www.medscape.com.*

Bea, Scott; Liebowitz, Michael; and Zamorski, Mark. "Managing Generalized Anxiety Disorder." *Patient Care 33 (*August 15, 1999):97-119.

Borkovec, T.D.; and Ruscio, A.M. "Psychotherapy for Generalized Anxiety Disorder." PubMed Website. *Journal of Clinical Psychiatry* 62 (2001), Suppl 11:37-42. *www.ncbi.nlm.nih.gov.*

Broocks, A.; Bandelow, B.; Pekrun, G.; George A.; Meyer, T.; Bartmann, U.; Burns, Steve; Burns, Kimberley; and Nickens, Wayne. "How to Deal with Overstress." Health Education Website. *www.teachhealth.com/dealwith.html.*

Carter, C.S.; Servan-Schreiber, D.; and Perlstein, W.M. "Anxiety Disorders and the Syndrome of Chest Pain with Normal Coronary Arteries: Prevalence and Pathophysiology." *Journal of Clinical Psychiatry* 58 (1997), Suppl 3:70-3. *www.medscape.com.*

Connor, K.M.; Davidson, J.R.; Sutherland, S.; and Weisler, R. "Social Phobia: Issues in Assessment and Management." *Epilepsia* 40 (1999) Suppl 6;S60-5. *www.ncbi.nlm.nih.gov.*

"Cycle of Violence to Children and Animals." Orlando Humane Society Website. *www.ohs-spca.org/violence.htm.*

Damecour, C.L.; and Charron, M. "Hoarding: A Symptom, Not a Syndrome." *Journal of Clinical Psychiatry* 59(May 1998):267-72; quiz 273. *www.medscape.com.*

Daniels, Colin Y. "Panic Disorder." *EMedicine Journal* 3 (February 1, 2002).

Drummond, Edward. *Benzo Blues: A Groundbreaking Program for Overcoming Anxiety Without Tranquilizers.* New Hampshire: Sea Coast Mental Health Center, 1998.

"Facts About Generalized Anxiety Disorder." DrKoop.com Website. *www.drkoop.com.*

"Facts About Panic Disorder." The National Institutes of Health and DrKoop.com Website. *www.drkoop.com.*

"Family Context Variables and the Development of Self-Regulation in College Students." *Adolescence* 33(1998):17-31. *www.ncbi.nlm.nih.gov/entrez/query.*

Flament, M.F.; Godart, N.T.; Fermanian, J.; and Jeammet, P. "Predictive Factors of Social Disability in Patients with Eating Disorders." *Eating and Weight Disorders* 6(June 2001):99-106. *www.ncbi.nlm.nih.gov.*

Foa, E.B. "Trauma and Women: Course, Predictors, and Treatment." Medscape Medline Website. *Journal of Clinical Psychiatry* 58 (1997), Suppl 9:25-8. *www.medscape.com*

"Generalized Anxiety Disorder." The Anxiety Panic Internet Resource Website. *www.algy.com/anxiety/gad.html.*

Goodman, W.K. "Obsessive-Compulsive Disorder: Diagnosis and Treatment." *Journal of Clinical Psychiatry* 60 (1999), Suppl 18:27-32. *www.medscape.com.*

Govaker, David; and Rakel, Robert. "Early Detection of Mental Illness." *American Academy of Family Physicians Video CME Program. (*1999) Annual Clinical Focus, p. 8.

Hahn, Rhoda; Albers, Lawrence; and Reist, Christopher. "Panic Disorder." *www.medical-library.org.*

Health Education; Stress, Depression, Anxiety, Drug Use. Health Education Website. *www.teachhealth.com.*

"Heart Disease." Dean Ornish segment on *Oprah*, March 14, 2002.

Henning, Cathleen. "Could Your Panic Be Anger?" About.com Website. *www.About.com.*

Hidalgo, R.B.; and Davidson, J.R. "Generalized Anxiety Disorder. An Important Clinical Concern." PudMed Website. *Medical Clinics of North America* 85(May 2001):691-710. *www.ncbi.nlm.nih.gov.*

Hillmer-Vogel, U.; and Ruther, E. "Comparison of Aerobic Exercise, Clomipramine, and Placebo in the Treatment of Panic Disorder." *American Journal of Psychiatry* 155(1998):603-9. Medscape Medline Website. *www.medscape.com.*

Hirschfeld, R.M. "Panic Disorder: Diagnosis, Epidemiology, and Clinical Course." *Journal of Clinical Psychiatry* 57 (1996), Suppl 10:3-8. *www.medscape.com.*

Holcomb, Betty. *Not Guilty! The Good News for Working Mothers.* New York: Touchstone, 2000.

Holmes, T.; and Rahe, R. "Life Change and Illness Susceptibility. In B.P. Dohrenwend and B.S. Dohrenwend (eds) *Stressful Life Events: Their Nature and Effects.* New York: Wiley, 1974:45-72.

Holmes, T.H.; and Rahe, R.H. "The Social Readjustment Rating Scale." *Journal of Psychosomatic Research* II (1967):213-218.

Ireys, H.T.; Chernoff, R.; DeVet, K.A.; and Kim, Y. "Maternal Outcomes of a Randomized Controlled Trial of a Community-Based Support Program for Families of Children with Chronic Illnesses." *Archives of Pediatrics & Adolescent Medicine* 155(July 7, 2001):763-4. *www.ncbi.nlm.gov.*

"Job-Stress-Induced Illnesses: Are You at Risk?" *Prevention* Website. March 1, 2001. *www.prevention.com.*

Johnson, H.D.; LaVoie J.C.; Spenceri, M.C.; and Mahoney-Wernli, M.A. "Peer Conflict Avoidance: Associations with Loneliness, Social Anxiety, and Social Avoidance." *Psychological Reports* 88 (February 2001):227-35. PubMed Website. *www.ncbi.nlm.nih.gov.*

Johnson, Margaret T. "Anxiety." *www.medical-library.org.*

Kaplan, Harold I.; Sadock, Benjamin J.; and Grebb, Jack A. *Synopsis of Psychiatry, Behavioral Sciences Clinical Psychiatry, 7th ed.* Baltimore, Maryland: Williams & Wilkins, 1994.

Kelley, William N. *Textbook of Internal Medicine.* New York: Lippincott-Raven, 1997.

Khouzam, Hani Raoul. "Obsessive-Compulsive Disorder: What to Do If You Recognize Baffling Behavior." *Postgraduate Medicine* 106 (December 1999):133-141.

Kobasa, S. "Stressful Life Events, Personality, and Health: An Inquiry into Hardiness." *Personality and Social Psychology* 37 (1979):1-11.

Kobasa, S.; Maddi, S.; and Kahn, S. "Hardiness and Health: A Prospective Study." *Journal of Personality and Social Problems,* 42 (1982):168-177.

Kraaimaat, F. "Group Social Skills Training or Cognitive Group Therapy as the Clinical Treatment of Choice for Generalized Social Phobia?" *Journal of Anxiety Disorders* 14 (September 2000):437-51. Medscape Medline Website. *www.medscape.com.*

Levine, Hallie. "Beat the Number-One Women's Health Threat." *Self Magazine* (March 2002):102-103.

Lieb, R.; Wittchen, H.U.; Hofler, M.; Fuetsch, M.; Stein, M.B.; Merikangas, K.R. "Parental Psychopathology, Parenting Styles, and the Risk of Social Phobia in Offspring; a Prospective-Longitudinal Community Study." *Archives of General Psychiatry* 57 (September 2000):859-66. *www.medscape.com.*

Liebowitz, M.R. "Update on the Diagnosis and Treatment of Social Anxiety Disorder." *Journal of Clinical Psychiatry* 160, Suppl 18(1999):22-6. *www.medscape.com.*

"Life Skills for Vocational Success." Health handout. *www.workshopsinc.com/manual/Ch6H2.html.*

"Linking Animal Cruelty to Human Violence." *www.cfhs.ca/Programs/HumaneEducation/ViolenceLink/ccbackgrounder4.htm.*

Lipetz, J.; and Kruse, R.J. "Injuries and Special Concerns of Female Figure Skaters." *Clinics in Sports Medicine* 19 (April 2000):369-80. *www.ncbi.nlm.nih.gov.*

Magee, W.J., Eaton, W.W.; Wittchen, H.U.; McGonagle, K.A.; and Kessler, R.C. "Agoraphobia, Simple Phobia, and Social Phobia in the National Comorbidity Survey." *Archives of General Psychiatry* 53 (February 1996):159-68. *www.medscape.com.*

Major, B.; Cozzarelli, C.; Cooper, M.L.; Zubek, J.; Richards, C.; Wilhite, M.; and Gramzow, R.H. "Psychological Responses of Women After First-Trimester Abortion." *Archives of General Psychiatry* 57 (August 2000):777-84. *www.medscape.com.*

Mann, Denise. "Meditation Does Ease Stress." MSN Website, 8 August 2001. *content.health.msn.com/content/article.*

Marer, Eva. "Knitting: The New Yoga." *Health Magazine* 16 (March 2002).

Markway, Barbara G.; and Markway, Gregory P. *Painfully Shy: How to Overcome Social Anxiety and Reclaim Your Life*. New York: St. Martin's Press, 2001.

Masia, C.L.; Klein, R.G.; Storch, E.A.; and Corda, B. "School-Based Behavioral Treatment for Social Anxiety Disorder in Adolescents: Results of a Pilot Study." *Journal of the American Academy of Child & Adolescent Psychiatry* 40 (July 2001);780-6.

Morris, T.L. "Childhood Anxiety Disorders: Etiology, Assessment, and Treatment in the New Millennium." *Current Psychiatry Reports* 3 (August 2001):267-72. *www.ncbi.nlm.nih.gov.*

Murphy, Bernadette. *Zen and the Art of Knitting: Exploring the Links Between Knitting, Spirituality, and Creativity*. Adams Media Corp. (September 2002).

"Panic Disorder." The Anxiety Panic Internet Resource Website. *www.algy.com/anxiety/panic.html.*

Papousek, M.; and von Hofacker, N. "Persistent Crying in Early Infancy: A Non-Trivial Condition of Risk for the Developing Mother-Infant Relationship." *Child Care Health Development* 24 (September 1998):395-424. *www.ncbi.nlm.nih.gov.*

"Post-Traumatic Stress Disorder." DrKoop.com Website. Women's Health Conditions. *www.drkooop.com/dyncon/article*.

Pozuelo, Leopoldo; Ross, Jerilyn; and Sussman, Norman. "The Anxiety Spectrum: Which Disorder Is It?" *Patient Care* 33 (15 August 1999); pp. 73-93.

Prensner, J.D.; Yowler, C.J.; Smith, L.F.; Steele, A.L.; and Fratianne, R.B. "Music Therapy for Assistance with Pain and Anxiety Management in Burn Treatment." *Journal of Burn Care & Rehabilitation* 22 (January-February 2001):83-8. PubMed Website. *www.ncbi.nlm.nih.gov*.

"PTSD and Community Violence." DrKoop.com Website. *www.drkoop.com/dyncom/article*.

"Rages and Refusals. Managing the Many Faces of Adolescent Anxiety." PubMed Website. August 22, 2001. *Canadian Family Physician* 47 (May 2001):1023-30. *www.ncbi.nlm.nih.gov*.

Rahe, R.; Lundberg, U.; Theorell, T.; and Bennett, L. "The Social Readjustment Rating Scale: A Comparative Study of Swedes and Americans." *Journal of Psychosomatic Research* 51 (1971):241-249.

Reuter, M.A.; Scaramella, L.; Wallace, L.E.; and Conger, R.D. "First Onset of Depressive or Anxiety Disorders Predicted by the Longitudinal Course of Internalizing Symptoms and Parent-Adolescent Disagreements." *Archives of General Psychiatry* 56 (August 1999):726-32. *www.medscape.com*.

Rosenbaum, J.F.; Moroz, G.; and Bowden, C.L. "Clonazepam in the Treatment of Panic Disorder with or without Agoraphobia: a Dose-Response Study of Efficacy, Safety, and Discontinuance." *Journal of Clinical Psychopharmacology* 17 (October 1997):390-400. *www.medscape.com*.

Rosenbaum, Jerrold F. "Panic Disorder in the Office or Emergency Department." *Emergency Medicine* 31 (November 1999):96-102.

Rutherford, Eleanor J. "Panic Attacks and Panic Disorder." *www.medical-library.org*.

Schneider, L.S. "Overview of Generalized Anxiety Disorder in the Elderly." *Journal of Clinical Psychiatry* 57, Suppl 7 (1996):34-45. *www.medscape.com*.

"School-Based Behavioral Treatment for Social Anxiety Disorder in Adolescents: Results of a Pilot Study." PubMed Website. *Journal of the American Academy of Child & Adolescent Psychiatry* 40 (July 2001):780-6. *www.ncbi.nlm.nih.gov*.

Scott, J.T.; Entwistle, V.A.; Sowden, A.J.; Watt, I. "Communicating with Children and Adolescents about Their Cancer (Cochrane Review)." *Cochrane Database System Review* 1 (2001). PubMed Website. *www.ncbi.nlm.nih.gov*.

Sheehan, David V. *The Anxiety Disease*. New York: Bantam Books, 1983.

Shelton, Richard C. "Remission of Anxiety-Related Disorders." *The Journal of Clinical Psychiatry* 62, Suppl 12 (2001).

"Social Phobia." DrKoop.com Website. National Cancer Institute. *www.drkoop.com/dyncon.article*.

Stanford, Elizabeth K. "Panic Disorder." *www.medical-library.org*.

Stein, M.B.; Chartier, M.J.; Hazen, A.L.; Kroft, C.D.; Chale, R.A.; Cote, D.; and Walker, J.R. "Paroxetine in the Treatment of Generalized Social Phobia; Open-Label Treatment and Double-Blind Placebo-Controlled Discontinuation." *Journal of Clinical Psychopharmacology* 16 (June 1996);218-22. *www.medscape.com*.

Stein, M.B.; McQuaid, J.R.; Laffaye, C.; and McCahill, M.E. "Social Phobia in the Primary Care Medical Setting." *Journal of Family Practice* 48 (July 1999):514-9. Medscape Medline Website. *www.medscape.com*.

Stewart, William. *Controlling Anxiety*. Oxford, United Kingdom: How To Books Ltd., 2000.

Strage, A.A. "Family Context Variables and Development of Self-Regulation in College Students." *Adolescence* 33 (Spring 1998):17-31. *www.ncbi.nlm.nih.gov*.

Sullivan, Sherry; and Carraher, Shawn M. "Stress and Life Events: A Review of the Constructs and Measurement." *www.iusb.edu/~mwacad/sulliv~3.htm.*

Terr L.C.; Bloch, D.A.; Michel, B.A.; Shi H.; Reinhardt, J.A.; and Metayer, S. "Children's Symptoms in the Wake of Challenger: a Field Study of Distant-Trauma Effects." *American Journal of Psychiatry* 156 (October 1999):1536-44. *www.medscape.com.*

"The Cycle of Violence." *www.animal-lib.org.au/lists/violence/violence.shtml.* August 22, 2001.

"The Link Between Stress and Your Health." DrKoop.com Website. *www.drkoop.com.*

"The Social Readjustment Rating Scale." *fccj.org/~jwisner/life.html.*

"Treatment of Generalized Anxiety Disorder." DrKoop.com Website. *www.drkoop.com.*

"Treatment of Panic Disorder." DrKoop.com Website. *www.drkoop.com.*

"Twenty Tips to Tame Stress." DrKoop.com Website. *www.drkoop.com/dyncon/article.*

Wald, J.; and Taylor, S. "Efficacy of Virtual Reality Exposure Therapy to Treat Driving Phobia." *Journal of Behavior Therapy & Experimental Psychiatry* 31 (September-December 2000):249-57. *www.ncbi.nlm.nih.gov.*

Warshaw, M.G.; and Keller, M.B. "The Relationship Between Fluoxetine Use and Suicidal Behavior in 654 Subjects with Anxiety Disorders." *Journal of Clinical Psychiatry* 57 (April 1996):158-66.

"Ways of Handling Stress and Anxiety." Psychological Self-Help Website. *mentalhelp.net/psyhelp/chap5/chap51.htm.*

Web-chat with Dr. Michael Otto during the White House Conference on Mental Health, June 7, 1999. "Overview of Anxiety Disorders." *adaa.org/forprofessionals/events/chat_trans.htm.*

Weeks, H. "Taking the Stress Out of Stressful Conversations." *Harvard Business Review* 79 (July-August 2001):112-9, 146. *www.ncbi.nlm.nih.gov.*

Wellisch, D.K.; Hoffman, A.; Goldman, S.; Hammerstein, J.; Klein, K.; and Bell, M. "Depression and Anxiety Symptoms in Women at High Risk for Breast Cancer: Pilot Study of a Group Intervention." *American Journal of Psychiatry* 156 (October 1999):1644-5. *www.medscape.com.*

"What Is Obsessive-Compulsive Disorder, and Can It Be Treated?" *Family Practice Recertification* 22 (January 2000):47-48.

"What to Do If a Family Member Has an Anxiety Disorder." DrKoop.com Website. *www.drkoop.com.*

Woodman, Catherine L. "The Natural History of Generalized Anxiety Disorder: A Review." Medscape Website. *psychiatry.medscape.com.*

Zajecka, J. "Importance of Establishing the Diagnosis of Persistent Anxiety." *Journal of Clinical Psychiatry* 58 (1997) 9-13; discussion 14-5. Medscape Medline Website. *www.medscape.com.*

Zal, H. Michael. "Five Herbs for Depression, Anxiety, and Sleep Disorders: Uses, Benefits, and Adverse Effects." *Consultant Magazine* 39 (December 1999):3343-3346.

Zalusky, S. "Infertility in the Age of Technology." *Journal of the American Psychoanalytic Association* 48 (2000):1541-62. PubMed Website. *www.ncbi.nlm.nih.gov.*

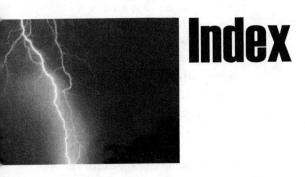

Index

About the Authors

JENNIFER SHOQUIST, M.D.: JENNIFER'S INTEREST IN HEALTH ISSUES began when she was attending the High School for the Performing and Visual Arts, while also interning at *Health & Fitness Magazine* in Houston, Texas. Since that time, she has gone on conquer her own anxiety attacks and complete her medical degree at the University of Texas Medical School at Houston. Today, she is a family practice physician who also serves as a health-issues resource for journalists. Accustomed to treating patients of all ages, she has called on her knowledge and experiences in medicine to co-author a book on toilet training (*Potty Training For Dummies*, June 2002), and a reference book on STDs (*The Encyclopedia of Sexually Transmitted Diseases*, 2003). She and Diane Stafford wrote for 2002 publication, *Migraines For Dummies*.

Dr. Shoquist and her husband, Robert San Luis, live in Houston with their shih-tzus Lucy and Sophie. Their first baby is due in September 2002. Jennifer's special interests include travel, dogs, reading, exercise, and nutrition.

DIANE STAFFORD: DIANE'S WRITING CAREER BEGAN AS A 9-YEAR-OLD poet, who went on to become editor of her high school newspaper, and then snagged a great summer job as a speechwriter for the space program, while she was attending college at Sam Houston State in Huntsville, Texas. After graduating, she taught journalism and English, and then went on to a second career as a writer/editor, serving as editor-in-chief of *Health & Fitness Magazine, Texas Woman Magazine, Houston Home & Garden, Dallas-Fort Worth Home & Garden, Philanthropy in Texas*, and *Latin Music.* Also an entrepreneur, Stafford co-owned *Health & Fitness* and helped with startups of the magazine in New Orleans, Philadelphia, Miami, and Atlanta. She has won awards for health writing, and has written hundreds of articles. She edits books for Arte Publico Press.

Stafford has co-authored *Potty Training For Dummies, Migraines For Dummies, The Encyclopedia of Sexually Transmitted Diseases, and Close Encounters: 100 Tips for Achieving the Intimacy You Desire* (the latter with co-authors Cari La Grange and Marvin Stone, M.D.). She has written one novel, *Tilted Heart,* for Kensington.

Diane lives with her husband, David Garrett, in Houston, where she is a well-known writer and a community volunteer for Casa de Esperanza de los Ninos, and the Emergency Aid Coalition Clothes Center. Jennifer Shoquist is Diane's beloved daughter.

Much like her co-author, Diane had to find ways to cope with anxiety, which helped her write this book packed with ideas for curbing anxiety in 100 situations.